THE BEST OF
D. L. MOODY

THE BEST OF
D. L. MOODY

Sixteen Sermons by the
Great Evangelist

Edited by
WILBUR M. SMITH

MOODY PRESS • Chicago

© 1971 by
THE MOODY BIBLE INSTITUTE
OF CHICAGO

Library of Congress Catalog Card Number: 75-143467

ISBN: 0-8024-0495-2

Second Printing, 1973

CONTENTS

The Admiration and Love of One Great Preacher for Another

UNDOUBTEDLY the two preachers of the gospel who could consistently draw the largest audiences in the English-speaking world in the next to the last decade of the nineteenth century (1880-1889) were Charles H. Spurgeon and Dwight L. Moody. Recently in rereading the fourth volume of the great autobiographical work of Mr. Spurgeon, I came upon a remarkable tribute by D. L. Moody to Mr. Spurgeon which I do not recall ever having seen before. This tribute was uttered by Mr. Moody in the Metropolitan Tabernacle in June, 1884, at a great celebration of the fiftieth anniversary of Mr. Spurgeon. I thought in this volume where we have gathered together some of Mr. Moody's sermons it would not be out of place to bring this glowing tribute of one preacher to another to the attention of this generation.

Mr. Spurgeon has said, to-night, that he has felt like weeping. I have tried to keep back the tears, but I have not succeeded very well. I remember, seventeen years ago, coming into this building a perfect stranger. Twenty-five years ago, after I was converted, I began to read of a young man preaching in London with great power, and a desire seized me to hear him, never expecting that, some day, I should myself be a preacher. Everything I could get hold of in print that he ever said, I read. I knew very little about religious things when I was converted. I did not have what he has had, a praying father. My father died before I was four years old. I was thinking of that, to-night, as I saw Mr. Spurgeon's venerable father here by his side. He has the advantage of me in that respect, and he perhaps got an earlier start than he would have got if he had not had that praying father. His mother I have not met; but most good men have praying mothers, God bless them! In 1867, I made my way across the

7

sea; and if ever there was a sea-sick man for fourteen days, I
was that one. The first place to which I came was this building. I was told that I could not get in without a ticket, but
I made up my mind to get in somehow, and I succeeded. I
well remember seating myself in this gallery. I recollect the
very seat, and I should like to take it back to America with
me. As your dear Pastor walked down to the platform, my
eyes just feasted upon him, and my heart's desire for years
was at last accomplished. It happened to be the year he
preached in the Agricultural Hall. I followed him up there,
and he sent me back to America a better man. Then I began
to try and preach myself, though at the time I little thought
I should ever be able to do so. While I was here, I followed
Mr. Spurgeon everywhere; and when, at home, people asked
if I had gone to this and that cathedral, I had to say "No,"
and confess I was ignorant of them; but I could tell them
something about the meetings addressed by Mr. Spurgeon.
In 1872, I thought I would come over again to learn a little
more, and I found my way back to this gallery. I have been
here a great many times since, and I never come into the
building without getting a blessing to my soul. I think I have
had as great a one here to-night as at any other time I have
been in this Tabernacle. When I look down on these orphan
boys, when I think of the 600 servants of God who have gone
out from the College to preach the gospel, of the 1,500 or
2,000 sermons from this pulpit that are in print, and of the
multitude of books that have come from the Pastor's pen,
(Scripture says, "Of making many books there is no end,"
and in his case it is indeed true,) I would fain enlarge upon
all these good works, but the clock shows me that, if I do, I
shall not get to my other meeting in time. But let me just say
this, if God can use Mr. Spurgeon, why should He not use
the rest of us, and why should we not all just lay ourselves at
the Master's feet, and say to Him, "Send me, use me"? It is
not Mr. Spurgeon who does the work, after all; it is God. He
is as weak as any other man apart from his Lord. Moses was
nothing, but Moses' God was almighty. Samson was nothing
when he lost his strength; but when it came back to him,
then he was a mighty man; and so, dear friends, bear in mind
that, if we can just link our weakness to God's strength, we

can go forth, and be a blessing in the world. Now, there are others to speak, and I have also to hasten away to another meeting, but I want to say to you, Mr. Spurgeon, "God bless you! I know that you love me, but I assure you that I love you a thousand times more than you can ever love me, because you have been such a blessing to me, while I have been a very little blessing to you. I have read your sermons for twenty-five years. You are never going to die. John Wesley lives more to-day than when he was in the flesh; Whitefield lives more today than when he was on this earth; John Knox lives more today than at any other period of his life; and Martin Luther, who has been gone over three hundred years, still lives." Bear in mind, friends, that our dear brother is to live for ever. We may never meet together again in the flesh; but, by the blessing of God, I will meet you up yonder.

Doctoral Theses Regarding D. L. Moody

"Moody is now sufficiently well embedded in history to be the subject of Ph.D. dissertations. There was one done at the University of Wisconsin in 1942, by B. F. Huber, entitled 'D. L. Moody, Salesman of Salvation.' Rollin W. Quimby wrote another at the University of Michigan in 1951, called 'Dwight L. Moody: An Examination of the Historical Conditions and Rhetorical Factors Which Contributed to His Effectiveness as a Speaker,' Richard Curtis submitted a doctoral dissertation at Purdue Univeristy on 'The Pulpit Speaking of Dwight L. Moody,' dated 1954. The Huber work is available on an interlibrary-loan basis, and the other two are on microfilm. I have only looked hastily at Huber's dissertation, but I read the other two carefully. They are limited in scope and standard-seminar in style. I have not seen an earlier dissertation on Moody done by Vernon F. Schwalm at the University of Chicago in 1915. As for other unpublished sources on Moody's life, there is a manuscript work, 'Moody of Northfield,' by Elmer W. Powell, a Philadelphia minister who has made a lifelong study of Moody and collected a great deal of Moodyana for the library of the Crozier Theological Seminary at Chester, Pennsylvania. Mrs. Emma Moody Fitt Powell, Moody's granddaughter, who resides in Northfield, also has some personal papers. I have not seen them or the Powell work."

BERNARD A. WEISBERGER, *They Gathered at the River* (Boston: Little, Brown & Co., 1958) , p. 314.

INTRODUCTION

ONLY OF DWIGHT L. MOODY of the great American preachers of the nineteenth century is it true that his printed sermons have been continuously available for almost a century, indeed since 1875. The only other great preacher of that century of which this is true is not an American but an Englishman, the great Charles H. Spurgeon. The publishing of Mr. Moody's sermons began in London (soon to be followed in America) with the title, *The London Discourses of Mr. D. L. Moody as Delivered in the Agricultural Hall and Her Majesty's Opera House.* In the preface of this volume of nearly 200 pages, we read that these discourses "were specially reported for the *Christian World* and have all, with the exception of five, been published in special extra numbers of that journal. They are verbatim reproductions of the addresses actually delivered by the celebrated American evangelist." The preface almost speaks prophetically when it says that "these discourses may be accepted as giving substantially the whole circle of Mr. Moody's teaching. They were repeated by the author in the four districts of the metropolis in which he labored as they had been previously in provincial towns of Great Britain, and also, we understand, in Chicago and other cities of the United States."

In the same year was published *Wondrous Love,* a series of fifteen messages, as well as shorter books, such as *The Prophet Daniel, The Right Kind of Faith, The Scarlet Thread,* and two addresses on heaven. In 1876 appeared the volume, *Glad Tidings* (504 pp.). In the next year, 1877, four large volumes appeared: *Great Joy,* (530 pp.); *Holding the Fort* (512 pp.); *"To All People"* (514 pp.); *New Sermons, Addresses, and Prayers* (705 pp.). Thus within two years there were published five volumes of

Moody's sermons (of course, some of them being duplicated) extending to 2,770 pages! The largest single volume of messages by Mr. Moody was that published in 1883, *The Gospel Awakening,* a volume of over 1,000 pages.

There were probably about eighty different *titles* of Mr. Moody's sermons and addresses published in that great quarter of a century during which he carried on his major work. By 1900 his sermon on heaven had sold 425,000 copies, and the volume, *The Way to God,* 435,000. Many of these volumes were brought out in London where the great first campaign was carried on before they appeared in America. Actually it would be almost impossible to construct a complete bibliography of Mr. Moody's printed sermons because scores of them were never copyrighted. For example, in the *American Catalogue* for 1881, seven volumes *about* Mr. Moody, some of them including a considerable amount of sermonic material are listed, but not a single volume exclusively devoted to his sermons is listed in this quite extensive work, because, for one reason or another, much of this sermonic material was not copyrighted. Some of these were just pamphlets of single sermons, such as *Christ All in All, Come Thou into the Ark, Full Assurance of Faith, The Way of Salvation, The Work of the Holy Spirit.* Some sermons appeared identically the same in a dozen or more different volumes. Some sermons appeared only once, as for example, in *The Gospel Awakening,* published in 1883, appear sermons not to be repeated in any other volume, as those on 1 Corinthians 18:2; Isaiah 26:4; Mark 10:21; 1 Corinthians 8:3; 15:49, etc. Sometimes the same sermon is given more than one title. · His sermon on Luke 4:18-19 is sometimes entitled "Secret Power," and sometimes "Power from on High." So also his famous sermon, "Come," is sometimes entitled "A Chime of Gospel Bells." Some of Mr. Moody's sermons appeared in periodicals that never found their way into his separately published volumes, as for example,. in the *Northfield Echoes* for 1897 are two sermons I have never seen in any volume of his sermons, "On the Road to Emmaus," and "The Seven Walks in Ephesians." If my study of this material is more or less complete, then as far as the publication of Mr. Moody's sermons indicate he preached from 160 texts, of which 119 were from the New Testament, and in addition, on about 96 different subjects, making a total of perhaps something over 260 different sermons preached during that quarter of a century, some of them sixty or seventy times, on both sides of the Atlantic, and some of them only once. Among the latter was his great sermon upon the sudden death of his beloved co-helper, P. P. Bliss, on the text, "Be thou also Ready" (appearing in *The Gospel Awakening*, pp. 553-60) .

John Wesley in his *Journal* has a most interesting statement about the reasonableness of preaching sermons over and over again.

> I went to Tiverton. I was musing here on what I heard a good man say long since: "Once in seven years I burn all my sermons; for it is a shame if I cannot write better sermons now than I could seven years ago." Whatever others can do, I really cannot. I cannot write a better sermon on the Good Steward than I did seven years ago; I cannot write a better on the Great Assize, than I did twenty years ago; I cannot write a better on the Use of Money than I did nearly thirty years ago; nay, I know not that I can write a better on the Circumcision of the Heart than I did five-and-forty years ago. Perhaps, indeed, I may have read five or six hundred books more than I had then, and may know a little more history, or natural philosophy, than I did; but I am not sensible that this has made any essential addition to my knowledge in divinity. Forty years ago I knew and preached every Christian doctrine which I preach now.

THE OBJECTIVES IN THE PREACHING OF D. L. MOODY

Anyone who has even a nominal acquaintance with the printed sermons of D. L. Moody would surely acknowledge that the one great major objective in all of his preaching was *the salvation of the souls of men and women.* The very titles of his sermons illustrate this, as his famous one, "Ye Must Be Born Again," and those constantly preached on "Regeneration," "Grace," "How to Be Saved," "The Gospel," "Christ's Mission to the World," "The Death of Christ," "What Will Ye Do with Jesus?", "The Blood," "Christ the Water of Life," "Christ the Bread of Life," "Instantaneous Salvation," "The Atonement," "Come into the Ark," the compassionate sermon on some of the great passages in which the word *Come* appears, etc. As a corollary to the preaching of the gospel of salvation would be the theme so often seen in Mr. Moody's sermons—warning and exhortation. Some of these may be found in almost any volume of his sermons, such as "Sowing and Reaping," "Excuses," "Weighed and Wanting," "Be Not Deceived," "Son, Remember," etc.

The second major area of thought in Mr. Moody's preaching for a quarter of a century was encouraging Christians to engage in work for the Lord, as seen in his sermons on "Courage and Enthusiasm," "To Every Man His Work" (Mk 13:34), "Power for Service" (Jn 7:37), "The Soul Winner," "Working for Christ" (Ac 7:52), "Christians Are Not to Faint," etc.

No great preacher of the nineteenth century used illustrations so frequently and so forcefully as Dwight L. Moody. Sometimes two-thirds of an entire sermon would consist only of a series of illustrations. Many of these were drawn from his own experiences, in visiting the homes of his church members (in his younger days), in his work as chaplain on the battlefields of the Civil War, in his frequent visits to prisons, etc. Some illustrations were drawn from the experiences of his friends, some from his own reading, and some from historical events of his and former generations. The reason he could draw so heavily upon his own experiences is because he had many rich experiences to draw upon. He was constantly at work for the Lord; he was interested in the welfare of others; he had a great group of loyal active Christian friends around him; he was sensitive to the needs of others.

He does not, I believe, very often refer to his own domestic life, which was a happy one indeed. He does tell about his efforts to teach his young son the meaning of faith, and in detail he describes his mother's joy when his wayward brother returned after years of absence. Rarely does he refer in his preaching to his beloved companion, Mrs. Moody. Though he often talked about the wonderful influence in his early life of his Sunday school teacher in Boston, Moody did not, I think, speak frequently of his own inner experiences as a great preacher of the gospel. One exception was his dramatically narrated story of how his attention was drawn to the study of the life of Noah through the visit of a layman, who talked to him in his early days of preaching.

It would seem that Mr. Moody used more illustrations of death-bed scenes than of any other one specific experience of men and women. He often remarked that from early life he knew the fear of death, though Christ later delivered him from this. Some-times, especially in his sermon on the compassion of Jesus, Moody would introduce one illustration after another of deathbed scenes, many of which he himself witnessed. (See this reprinted in *Echoes from the Pulpit and Platform* by Charles F. Goss.) I doubt if such illustrations would be very effective today, but they certainly were effective as Mr. Moody used them in that final quarter of the nineteenth century.

One of the most effective stories that Mr. Moody ever used was that of the director of a prison reading out the name of Reuben Johnson (to the assembled prisoners) to whom the governor had given a pardon, and how long it took to dawn on this man that there really was awaiting a pardon for him, if he would step out from the other hundreds of prisoners and come forward and re-ceive it. The story of the bankrupt soldier who was found asleep from sheer exhaustion after he had listed his gambling debts, and was found by the Czar of Russia, who left a line telling the unawakened soldier that he would pay these debts is unforget-table. Some sermons had almost no illustrations, as the one on the second birth; sometimes a single illustration would be con-tinued for two pages, and often more than half a sermon would be devoted to stories—most of them actual events, though occa-sionally he would draw an imaginary picture.

Inasmuch as this has seldom been seen by anyone of this gener-ation, unless they have made a special study of Mr. Moody's ser-mons, I would like to quote here in its entirety, an autobiographi-cal passage in which Mr. Moody speaks so movingly of the long absence of his brother from the home at Northfield and his final return:

> Let me tell you a little incident that happened in our own family to illustrate God's willingness to receive sinners. The first thing I remember in my life was the death of my father. He died before I was four years old. One beautiful day in

June he fell suddenly dead on the floor, and his sudden death gave me such a shock that I have never forgotten it. It made an impression on my young mind that followed me through life. I can't remember the funeral. The only thing I remember of my father was his sudden death. The next thing I remember was that my mother was laid away upon a sick bed; and the third thing—for afflictions don't come generally singly —was that my oldest brother became a prodigal and ran away. I well remember how that mother mourned for that boy. I well remember away back in my early childhood how that mother thought of that boy, and I used to think mother loved him more than all the rest of us put together—and I think she did; it was the love of pity. I remember the cold winter nights, as we used to sit round the old family fireside, and we talked to our mother about our father—how he acted and what he used to do, and we would sit for hours and hear mother talk of him; but if we mentioned that elder brother all would be silent. Mother never heard his name mentioned without tears coming; and some nights when there would be gales of wind, mother didn't sleep at all. She thought, "He may be on the sea, and in that gale. He may be in trouble"; and these nights she was ever praying for him.

THE MOTHER'S CRY

I remember some nights waking past midnight and hearing a voice in my mother's chamber; and I heard that mother weeping and saying, "O God, send back my boy. O God, shelter him and protect him, and take care of him." That was her cry. And when there came a day when the nation returned thanks for the harvest, a day when all the family comes together, mother used to say to us and raise our hopes, "Perhaps he will come back to-day," and his chair was kept vacant, and the place at the table. And he never returned. We wrote to different parts of the country as we grew up: If we found any paper that had a man named with the name of our brother, we would write to see if it was our brother. I remember once finding a notice in a Californian paper of a man bearing that name, and I thought it was him. I wrote out there, and was very much disappointed at receiving a letter telling me he wasn't the man. Yet mother prayed on and hoped on, seemingly against hope, until the hair once black turned grey, and the step once firm began to tremble, and I could see grief carrying that dear mother into an untimely grave. How my heart used to bleed for her!

THE PRODIGAL'S RETURN

One day, as she was sitting in her little cottage, her two youngest children, that were infants when brother left home, and were now grown up almost to manhood and womanhood, sitting at the table with her, a stranger appeared at the gate, and he came up to the east piazza and stood with his arms folded, looking on that mother he hadn't seen for years. Mother didn't recognize her boy; but when she saw those tears rolling down over the long black beard, through those tears she saw it was her long-lost boy, and when she saw it was her lost boy she said, "Oh, my son, come in." And he says with his arms folded, "No, mother; I will not come across your threshold until you forgive me." Sinner, do you believe she was ready to forgive him? She didn't wait for him to come in, but ran to the door, threw her arms round his neck and wept for joy. The dead was alive, the lost was found, the wanderer was come home, and the joy it gave that mother, I cannot tell it to you. None but the mother that had the prodigal boy can realise that mother's joy. I cannot tell you what joy it gave us as a family; but it was nothing compared to the joy in heaven to-night, if you will only come home. Your Father wants you; and so come home this very night. He will receive every one of you if you will only come. May God help you to come now! May the Lord incline you to come, and you will find a warm welcome. He will give you a hearty response! Oh, may God incline you now to believe on the Lord Jesus Christ and to be saved!

There is a passage in the interesting volume, *Echoes from the Pulpit and Platform* by Dr. Charles F. Goss, who for five years was a pastor of Moody Church during Moody's lifetime. In it there are some interesting statistical matters concerning Moody's preaching which, I think, might interest many of the readers of this volume.

In passages of the same length (about 530 words chosen at random from printed sermons) I have estimated that Mr.

Moody uttered thirty-six sentences; Bushnell, twenty; Spurgeon, twenty-one; Lacordaire, fifteen; Chalmers, nine.

It would seem as if such brevity would have rendered his speech unmusical; but this was far from being the case. There was a flow and smoothness to its movement which gave an actual pleasure to the ear. In passages of intense excitement the sentences possessed an explosive quality suggesting a pack of fire crackers set off by accident; but after he had gained control of his vocal organs, and of his inflammable emotions, there was nothing of this character.

As the brevity of his sentences was a marked characteristic of his style, so was that of his words. His vocabulary was exceedingly limited; but exactly adapted to his use. Among his words those of three or four syllables are rare. He seemed incapable of uttering them.

In a page of 530 words, 400 contained only a single syllable, and most of them are Anglo Saxon. Many of his longer words were terribly shortened, terminals like "ing" being almost invariably abbreviated to "in." B. F. Jacobs used to say that D. L. Moody was the only man living who could say "Jerusalem" in two syllables.

There were certain passages in some of his sermons where, judged by the effect they produced, it must be said he rose to a sublime eloquence. I heard him preach his sermon on "Elijah" in the city of Detroit, when it appeared to me that supernatural things were actually occurring in the room. The line of demarcation between the real and the imaginary seemed broken down. That solemn hush had fallen upon the audience which rests upon the world before a thunder storm. You would have thought that every listener had been nailed to his seat. In the final outburst we actually beheld the chariot swoop down from heaven, the old man ascend, the blazing car borne through the still air; and when the impassioned orator uttered that piercing cry, "My father, my father, the chariot of Israel and the horsemen thereof!" the excitement was almost unbearable.

In a recent scholarly volume, *The Eighteenth Century Pulpit*, by Dr. James Downey there are some interesting statistics in relation to this matter of the number of sermons preached by great evangelists. George Whitefield (1714-1770) preached 18,000 sermons in thirty-five years, of which seventy-eight were published. By 1772 there had appeared twenty-eight collected editions of his sermons, five of which appeared in America. It is estimated that John Wesley (1703-1791) preached 40,000 sermons within sixty years. There were 133 sermons of Wesley published, eight of them after his death. Of these forty-four make up the *Standard Sermons,* the doctrinal standard of Methodism. Professor Downey says that these are "the only eighteenth century sermons which have been assured an audience in every generation since their publication."

A remarkable illustration of the tremendous power of persuasion that was exercised by Mr. Moody while preaching concerns his famous sermon on Deuteronomy 32:31. This was recorded many years ago in the *Evangelical Christian* by George Soltau and republished in a four-page leaflet. Since both of these items are practically unavailable today, I quote it in its entirety:

> Amongst the most remarkable scenes I have ever witnessed was one in East London during the visit of those beloved and honored men of God, Moody and Sankey, in the years 1883-84. The hall was pitched in the center of the dense working population of that quarter, where men by the hundred thousand work and live in workshops and factories. One Monday evening had been reserved for an address to atheists, skeptics, and free-thinkers of all shades.
>
> At that time Charles Bradlaugh, the champion of atheism, was at his zenith, and hearing of this meeting he ordered all the clubs he had formed to close for the evening, and all the members to go and take possession of the hall. They did so, and five thousand men marched in from all directions and occupied every seat. The platform was occupied by the clergy and workers.
>
> The service commenced earlier than usual, after the preliminary singing. Mr. Moody asked the men to choose their favorite hymns, which suggestion raised many a laugh, for atheists have no song or hymn. The meeting got well under way. Mr. Moody spoke from "Their rock is not our rock, our enemies themselves being the judges." He poured in a broadside of telling, touching incidents from his own experience of the deathbeds of Christians and atheists, and let the men be

the judges as to who had the best foundation on which to rest faith and hope. Reluctant tears were wrung from many an eye. The great mass of men, with the darkest, most determined defiance of God stamped upon their countenances, faced this running fire attacking them in their most vulnerable points, namely, their hearts and their homes; but when the sermon was ended one felt inclined to think nothing had been accomplished, for it had not appealed to their intellects, or reasoning faculties, and had convinced them of nothing.

At the close, Mr. Moody said, "We will rise and sing 'Only Trust Him,' and while we do so, will the ushers open all the doors, so that any man who wants to leave can do so; and after that we will have the usual inquiry meeting for those who desire to be led to the Saviour." I thought, all will stampede and we shall only have an empty hall. But instead, the great mass of five thousand men rose, sang, and sat down again, not one man vacating his seat.

What next? Mr. Moody then said, "I will explain four words—receive, believe, trust, take HIM." A broad grin pervaded all that sea of faces. After a few words upon "receive," he made the appeal, *"Who will receive Him?"* Just say, "I will." From the men standing round the edge of the hall came some fifty responses, but not one from the mass seated before him. One man growled "I can't," to which Mr. Moody replied, "You have spoken the truth, my man; glad you spoke. Listen, and you will be able to say 'I can' before we are through." Then he explained the word believe, and made his second appeal, "Who will say 'I will believe Him'?" Again some responded from the fringe of the crowd, till one big fellow, a leading club man, shouted "I won't." Dear Mr. Moody, overcome with tenderness and compassion, burst into broken, tearful words, half sobs, "It is 'I will,' or 'I won't' for every man in this hall tonight."

Then he suddenly turned the whole attention of the meeting to the story of the Prodigal Son, saying, *"The battle is on the will, and only there.* When the young man said 'I will arise,' the battle was won, for he had yielded his will; and on that point all hangs tonight. Men, you have your champion there in the middle of the hall, the man who said 'I won't'. I want every man here who believes that man is right to follow him, and to rise and say 'I won't'." There was perfect silence and stillness; all held their breath, till as no man rose, Moody burst out, "Thank God, no man says 'I won't.' Now, who'll say 'I will'?"

In an instant the Holy Spirit seemed to have broken loose upon that great crowd of enemies of Jesus Christ, and *five hundred men sprang to their feet,* their faces raining down with tears, shouting, "I will, I will," till the whole atmosphere was changed, and the battle was won. Quickly the meeting was closed, that personal work might begin, and from that night till the end of the week nearly two thousand men were swung out from the ranks of the foe into the army of the Lord, by the surrender of their will. They heard His "rise and walk," and they followed Him. The permanency of that work was well attested for years afterward, and the clubs never recovered their footing. God swept them away in His mercy and might by the gospel.

The Biblical Source of Mr. Moody's Sermons

From a careful listing of all the sermons of Mr. Moody that have appeared in book form is revealed that apart from the many sermons preached on subjects (rather than on texts) as his great sermons on "Grace," "The Love of God," "Heaven," etc., it would seem that Mr. Moody preached during the quarter of a century of his great ministry from 160 texts, of which 41 are in the Old Testament and 119 in the New Testament. A study of the location of these texts presents us with some interesting data. Mr. Moody had a great fondness for the book of Genesis, especially the two texts, "Where art thou?" (3:9) and that great invitation, "Come thou and all thy house into the ark" (7:1). Indeed, I have found his sermon on Genesis 3:9 in more volumes of sermons by Mr. Moody (nine of them) than I have found that of any other text in the Old Testament, Daniel 5:27 coming closest to this.

Yet from all the five books of the Pentateuch, and Joshua, Mr. Moody apparently preached from only nine texts—from the books of Samuel and Kings, six texts; one each from Job, Ecclesiastes, and Hosea; and three from the book of Jeremiah. The book that Mr. Moody loved most in the Old Testament Scriptures, and from which he preached most frequently, was Isaiah, from which he found sermons in ten different texts, especially from the latter part of the book relating to the sufferings of our Lord, chapters 53 and 55. It is interesting to note that Mr. Moody apparently did not preach from the books of Judges, Ruth, Chronicles, Ezra, Proverbs, Ezekiel, or from eleven of the minor prophets. In saying this, we must remember that not all the sermons Mr. Moody ever preached have appeared in book form. I am sure there are a number of sermons reported in the London evangelical weeklies, such as *The Christian* and *The Life of Faith,* and in many of our own journals of that era, which never reappeared in book form. To check all this material would be a worthy task which no one thus far has undertaken.

Of all the sources for sermonic material used by Mr. Moody, the portions from which he most frequently preached were the gospels and the book of Acts. If my index is correct, Mr. Moody preached from twenty different texts from the gospel of Luke, twenty texts from the gospel of John, seventeen from the gospel of Matthew, nine from the gospel of Mark, and twelve from the book of Acts. Most of the texts from Matthew's gospel were from 6:20–22:42 and most of those from the gospel of Mark in sections preceding the narrative of Holy Week. Of the twenty sermons preached from Luke, six of them are found in the first five chapters, twelve in the first fourteen chapters, and all but one of them in the narrative of Christ's ministry preceding the final week. What Mr. Moody loved most, probably, of all the synoptic records, was the story of the prodigal son. He himself once said, "Perhaps there is no subject in the Bible that takes hold of me with as great force as this subject of the wandering sinner: it enters deeply into my own life." Strange to say, he did not preach frequently from those passages which describe the last hours of our Lord's life, though he often preached on the blood of Christ. On the twenty texts from John's gospel, thirteen of them are found in the first seven chapters, and no printed sermon was preached from John 15–21.

In the New Testament, there were no sermons from 1 and 2 Thessalonians, 1 Timothy, and 2 Peter, and from the book of Revelation nothing from the great prophetic chapters: only one sermon from 3:17.

While Mr. Moody often preached on the second coming of Christ, he never seemed to be inclined to preach from what we might call prophetic passages. While he loved the book of Daniel, and possibly spoke more often from this book than from any other one book other than the gospels, yet, for example, when he preached from the ninth chapter, the sermon is on Daniel's prayer, not on the great prophecy of that chapter. As mentioned before, he did not preach at all from the book of Ezekiel, nor from the great prophetic passages of the book of Revelation. Even though many of his sermons are based upon verses in the synoptic gospels, Mr. Moody seemed to wholly pass by the accounts of our Lord's Olivet Discourse. The only text which he used from these passages was Mark 13:34 for his sermon "To Every Man His Work," found in innumerable volumes of his messages. This omission of preaching from these famous passages of prophecy is the more significant as Mr. Moody in his earlier years sat at the feet of some of the best Bible teachers of his generation, on both sides of the Atlantic, many of them Plymouth Brethren, who certainly would talk frequently about the prophetic significance of this age, and what has been commonly referred to as signs of the times. The one single exception that I know of, a clear reference to the prophetic significance of his age, is to be found in Mr. Moody's personally edited volume, *Bible Characters* (1888). In the chapter on his famous delineation of the character of Daniel entitled, "Thou Art the Head of Gold," Mr. Moody makes a statement which I do not recall finding anywhere else in his writings:

> I believe in the literal fulfilment, so far, of Daniel's God-given words; and in the sure fulfilment of the final prophecy of the "stone cut out of the mountain, without hands," that by and by shall grind the kingdoms of this world into dust, and bring in the kingdom of peace.
>
> Whilst the feet were of clay, there was some of the strength of the iron remaining in them. At the present day we have got down to the toes, and even to the extremities of these. Soon, very soon, the collision may occur; and then will come the end. The "stone cut out without hands" is surely coming— and it may be very soon.

What does Ezekiel say, prophesying within some few years of the time of this very vision?—"Remove the diadem, and take off the crown. . . . I will overturn, overturn, overturn; and it shall be no more, until he come whose right it is: and I will give it him."

What does St. Paul say?—"The appearing of our Lord Jesus Christ; which in his time he shall show, who is the blessed and only Potentate; the King of kings; and Lord of lords; . . . to whom be honor and power everlasting."

Yes, the Fifth Monarchy is coming: and it may be very soon. Hail, thou Fifth Monarch, who art to rule the world in righteousness, and sway the sceptre "from the river unto the ends of the earth." Shortly the cry, "Christ is come!" will be ringing through the earth. It is only a "little while." Cheer up, ye children of God; our King will be back by and by!

There are many articles scattered through British and American periodicals of the early part of our century describing the characteristics and effectiveness of Mr. Moody's preaching, which would be interesting to collect. Let me mention only one. A testimony in 1937 from Dr. Henry Sloan Coffin, then president of Union Theological Seminary, recalling a time when Mr. Moody was delivering his famous message on Daniel to a group of college students in the 1890s.

Mr. Moody, speaking in the name of the King, leaned over (the side of the pulpit) and said: "Oh, Dan'l, servant of the living God, is thy God whom thou servest continually able to deliver thee from the lions?" Then from this profound pit came the voice: "Oh, King, live forever. My God has sent his Angel and has stopped the lions' mouths."

There was nothing bizarre, nothing spectacular, nothing theatrical, nothing irreverent. This was the word of God, but it was so vivid to him that he made us feel that we were right on the spot.

There seems to me, though I have not noticed a reference to it in any studies of the ministry of Dwight L. Moody, that there is one single sentence in which St. Paul summarizes his work of preaching in Thessalonica that states perfectly the three great basic factors of Mr. Moody's preaching, "For our gospel came not unto you in word only, but also in power, and in the Holy Ghost, and in much assurance; as ye know what manner of men we were among you for your sake" (1 Th 1:5).

WILBUR M. SMITH

A STARTLING QUESTION

GENESIS 3:9

Preface

MR. MOODY had a particular fondness for the book of Genesis, and preached frequently from its earlier chapters. In fact, he preached more different sermons from the book of Genesis than from the other four books of the Pentateuch and Joshua combined.

In this sermon, illustrations play a prominent part. Indeed, the sermon opens with an illustration that forms one-twelfth of the entire message, and, as often, these illustrations are from the darker aspects of life. One relates to a drunkard, one to a dying man and his physician, one to the death of a child, one to a man hopelessly involved in debts resulting from gambling, etc.

In the text for this sermon in *London Discourses,* he closed with an illustration that occupies more than one-fifth of the entire text. In this text, Mr. Moody introduces something which was quite rare with him, that is, the dream of a little seven-year-old girl.

The text I am here using is from *Sermons, Addresses, and Prayers,* pp. 52-61. It may also be found in *Gospel Awakening* (1879), pp. 395-403; *Great Joy* (1879), pp. 60-72; *Great Redemption* (1889), pp. 271-84; *Holding the Fort,* pp. 115-21; *London Discourses* (1875), pp. 33-42; *Moody's Great Sermons* (1899), pp. 27-40; *Select Sermons* (1881), pp. 5-21.

A Startling Question

GENESIS 3:9, "Where art thou?"

YOU SEE I have got a very personal text this afternoon. All those ministers in this audience will bear me out in this statement, that it is the hardest kind of work to get their congregations to apply this text to themselves. When they hear it, one man passes it on to another, and away it goes, text and sermon. This afternoon, I want you to understand that it means me, you, and every one of us—that it points to us; that it applies to us personally—that it ought to come home to every soul here—to these merchants, to these ministers, to these reporters, to these great-hearted men, to these women, to these little boys and girls—as a personal question. It was the first question God put to man after his fall, and in the 6,000 years that have rolled away, all of Adam's children have heard it. It has come to them all. In the silent watches of the night, in the busy hours of the day, it has come upon us many a time—the question, "Where am I, whither am I going?" And I want you to look at it now as a personal question. So let us be solemn for a few minutes while we try to answer it. Some men look with great anxiety as to how they appear in the sight of their fellow-men. It is of very little account what the world thinks of us. The world is not worth heeding; public opinion is of very little account. We should not pay any attention to its opinion. "Where art thou going?" is the question that ought to trouble you. "What is to be your hereafter?" May the question strike home to us, and may a heart-searching take place in us, and the Holy Spirit search us, so that we may know before we sleep to-night where we are not in the sight of God, and where we are going to in eternity. I remember when preaching in New York City, at the Hippodrome, a man coming up to me and telling me a story that thrilled my soul. One night, he said, he had been gambling—had gambled away all the money he had. When he went home to the hotel that night he did not sleep much—half drunk, and with a sort of remorse for what he had done. The next morning happened to be Sunday. He got up, felt bad, couldn't eat anything, didn't touch his breakfast, was miserable, and thought about putting an end to his existence. That afternoon he took a walk up Broadway, and when he came to the Hippodrome he saw great crowds going in, and thought of entering too. But a policeman at the door told him he couldn't come in, as it was a woman's meeting. He turned from it and strolled on, came back to his hotel and had dinner. At night he walked up the street until he reached the Hippodrome again, and this time he saw a lot of men going in. When inside, he listened to the singing and heard the text: "Where art thou?" and he thought he would go out; he rose to go, and the text came upon his ears again, "Where art thou?" This was too personal, he thought; it was disagreeable, and he made for the door, but as he got to the third row from the entrance the words came to him again, "Where art thou?" He stood still, for the question had come to him with irresistible force, and God had found him right there. He went to his hotel and prayed all that night, and now he is a bright and shining light. And this young man, who was a commercial traveler, went back to the village in which he had been reared, and in which he had been one of the fastest young men—went back there, and went around among his friends and acquaintances and testified for Christ, as earnestly and beneficially for Him as his conduct had been against Him. I hope the text will find out some young man here who has strayed away from God, and come upon him with such force personally, as will turn him from his present course to take the offers of salvation. Won't you believe we are here for you? Won't you believe we are preaching for you? Won't you believe that this enterprise has been carried out for you, and that this assembly has been drawn together for you? And may you ask your heart solemnly and candidly this question: "Where art thou?"

I am going to divide this audience into three classes. Don't let this startle you, I am not going to make three divisions among you. The first class is the class who profess to be Christians. I don't know who you are, or whether you are sincere. It rests between you and God. The other class are the backsliders—those who have been good children, but who have turned their backs upon Him, and have gone into the regions of sin. And the next class is that one that has never been saved, who have never been born of the Spirit, who have never sought to reach Christ.

And now, my friends, as to you who profess to be Christians. We who profess to be Christians, are we living up to what we preach? God forgive me, I feel I am not doing as much as I should for Him. I don't except myself. You who profess to be Christians, this question is personal to you: "Where art thou?" Do you believe what you are preaching? Do you live the life you ought to be living as professed Christians? If you were doing this, tens of thousands of people would be converted in Chicago within thirty days. By your neglect to practice what you preach, men have got sick of you, the world has become tired of you. They say, if we really feel what we talk about and profess, we would be more earnest about their salvation. And I say they are right. If Christians felt as they should, every church in Chicago, every church in the North-west would be on fire for the salvation of souls. They are lukewarm. Is the Church to-day in its right position? Is it true to its teachings? Are we not mingling with the world in our professed Christian lives, so that the world has become tired of our shamming professions? If the world does not see us act according to our professions, they say Christianity is not real. Why, a young man, some time ago professed Christian, spoke to another young man upon the subject, and the Christian was answered with the words: "I don't believe a word of your Christianity; I don't believe a word of what you talk about; I don't believe your Bible." "You don't mean that?" asked the Christian. "Yes, I do," said the young man, "it's all a sham; you are all hypocrites." The Christian said to him, knowing he had a mother who was a professed Christian, "You don't mean to say that your mother is a hypocrite?" "Well, no," said the young fellow, not willing to admit his mother was one; "she is not exactly a hypocrite, but she don't believe what she professes. If she did, she would have talked to me about my soul long ago." That young man, my friends, had the best of it. And this is the condition of nine-tenths of us—we don't practice what we profess to believe. We have not really taken the cross of Christ; we have not put off the old man and taken on the new; we are not living truly in Christ Jesus, and the world is sick of us, and goes stumbling over us. If we don't practice in every particular the professions we make, and try to influence the lives of others, and lead the lives of Christians according to Christian precept, the world will go on stumbling over us. A few years ago, in a town somewhere in this State, a merchant died, and while he was lying a corpse I was told a story I will never forget. When the physician that attended him saw there was no chance for him here, he thought it would be time to talk about Christ to the dying man. And there are a great many Christians just like this physician. They wait till a man is just entering the other world—just till he is about nearing the throne, till the sands of life are about run out, till the death-rattle is in his throat—before they commence to speak of Christ. The physician stepped up to the dying merchant and began to speak of Jesus, the beauties of Christianity, and the salvation He had offered to all the world. The merchant listened quietly to him, and then asked him, "How long have you known of these things?" "I have been a Christian since I came from the East," he replied. "You have been a Christian so long and have known all this, and have been in my store every day. You have been in my home; have associated with me; you knew all these things, and why didn't you tell me before?" The doctor went home and retired to rest, but could not sleep. The question of the dying man rang in his ears. He could not explain why he had not spoken before, but he saw he had neglected his duty to his principles. He went back to his dying friend, intending to urge upon him acceptance of Christ's salvation, but when he began to speak to him the merchant only replied in a sad whisper, "Oh, why didn't you tell me before?" Oh, my friends, how many of us act like this physician. You must go to your neighbor and tell him who does not know Christ, of what He has done for us. If you do not tell the glad tidings, they are listening to the prompting of the devil, and we make people believe that Christianity is hypocrisy, and that Christ is not the Saviour of the world. If we believe it, shall we not publish it, and speak out the glorious truth to all for Christ—that He is the Redeemer of the world? Some time ago I read a little account that went through the press, and it burned into my soul. A father took his little child into the fields one day. He lay down while the child was amusing itself picking up little blades of grass and flowers. While the child was thus engaged the father fell asleep, and when he awoke, the first thought that occurred to him was, "Where is my child?" He looked around everywhere, but nowhere could he see the child. He looked all around the fields, over the mountains, but could not see her, and finally he came to a precipice and looked down among the stones and rocks, and there he saw his little child lying down at the bottom, and ran down, took the child up, and kissed it tenderly, but it was dead. He was filled with remorse, and accused himself of being the murderer of his child. And this story applies to Christians in their watchful care of their fellow-creatures.

It was not long ago that I heard of a mother making all sorts of fun and jeering at our preaching; not in Chicago, but in another town. She was laughing and scoffing at the meetings; she was scorning the preachers; and yet she had a drunken son. It might have been, if she had helped to support the meetings, the meetings would have been the means of saving that son from a drunkard's grave; and mothers and fathers here to-day, you have the responsibility upon you of turning the faces of your children toward Zion. Ah, my friends, it is a solemn question to you to-day, and may you ask yourself where you are in the sight of God. The next class I want to speak to for a few moments, for I can not help believing that in this assembly there must be a number of backsliders who have gone away from the wayside. You have probably come from an Eastern town to this one, and you have come to some church with a letter—to some Presbyterian, or Methodist, or Episcopalian church. And when you came to that church you did not find the love you expected; you didn't find the cordiality you looked for, and you did not go near it again. So you kept the letter in your pocket for weeks, for years; might have been thrown in your trunk, might have been burned up in the Chicago fire; and you have forgotten all about your church life, and the letter has disappeared. You lead an ungodly life, but you are not happy. I have traveled about a good deal in the last five years, and I never knew a man who had turned away from religion to be a happy man. That man's conscience is always troubling him. He may come to Chicago and become prosperous and wealthy, but his wealth and position in the world cannot fill his heart. If there is a poor backslider in this building to-day, let him come back. Hear the Voice that calls you to come back. There is nothing you have done which God is not ready and able to forgive. If there is a poor wanderer on the mountains of sin, turn right round and face Him. He will hear your transgressions, and forgive your backsliding, and take you to His loving bosom, and this will be a happy night to you. Look at the home of the backslider. No prayers, no family altar there. As in the days of Elijah, they have put up the image of Baal in the place of their God. They have no peace; their conscience troubles them; they know they are not bringing their family up as they should. Is not that the condition of a good many here to-day? Oh, backslider, you know what your life is, but what will be your eternity if you fight against the Lord, who is only waiting to do you good?

I heard of a young man who came to Chicago to sell his father's grain. His father was a minister somewhere down here. The boy arrived in Chicago and sold the grain; and when the time came for him to return home, the boy did not come. The father and mother were up all night, expecting to hear the sound of the wagon every minute, but they waited and waited, and still he did not come. The father became so uneasy that he went into the stable and saddled his horse and came to Chicago. When he reached here he found that his son had sold the grain, but had not been seen since the sale, and concluded that he was murdered. After making investigation, however, he found that the boy had gone into a gambling-house and lost all his money. After they had taken all his money from him they told him to sell his horse and wagon, and he would recover his money, which he did. He was like the poor man who came down from Jericho to Jerusalem, and who fell among thieves, and after they had stripped him of everything, cast him off. And a great many of you think as this young man thought. You think that rum-sellers and gamblers are your best friends, when they will take from you your peace, your health, your soul, your money—everything you have, and then run away. Well, the father, after looking about for him fruitlessly, went home and told his wife what he had learned. But he did not settle down, but just took his carpet-bag in his hand and went from one place to another, getting ministers to

let him preach for them, and he always told the congregation
that he had a boy dearer to him than life, and left his address
with them, and urged them if ever they heard anything about
his boy to let him know. At last, after going around a good deal,
he got on his track and learned that he had gone to California.
It was during the time of the gold excitement. He went home,
but he did not write a letter to him. No; he just arranged his
business affairs and started for the Pacific coast to find his boy.
This is but an illustration of what God has been doing for you.
There has not been a day, an hour, a moment, but God has been
searching for you. When the father got to San Francisco he got
permission to preach, and he had a notice put in the papers in
the hope that it might reach the mining districts, trusting that if
his son were there it might reach him. He preached a sermon on
the Sunday, and when he pronounced the benediction the audience went away. But he saw in a corner, one who remained.
He went up to him and found that it was his boy. He did not
reprimand him, he did not deliver judgment upon him, but put
his loving arms around him, drew him to his bosom, and took
him back to his home. This is an illustration of what God wants
to do to us, what He wants to do to-day. He offers us His love and
His forgiveness.

There is one peculiarity about a backslider. You must get
back to Him as you went away. It is you who have gone away
by turning, by leaving Him; not He by leaving you. And the
way to get back to Him is to turn your face toward Him, and He
will receive you with joy and forgiveness. There will be joy in
your heart and there will be joy in Heaven this afternoon if you
return to Him. If you treated God as a personal friend, there
would not be a backslider. A rule I have had for years is to treat
the Lord Jesus Christ as a personal friend. He is not a creed,
a mere empty doctrine, but it is He Himself we have. The moment we have received Christ we should receive Him as a friend.
When I go away from home I bid my wife and children good-
bye, I bid my friends and acquaintances good-bye, but I never
heard of a poor backslider going down on his knees and saying,
"I have been near You for ten years; Your service has become
tedious and monotonous; I have come to bid You farewell; good-

bye, Lord Jesus Christ." I never heard of one doing this. I will tell you how they go away; they just run away. Where are you, you backslider? Just look upon your condition during the past ten years. Have they been years of happiness? Have they been years of peace? Echo answers ten thousands times, "No." Return to Him at once; never mind what your past has been, He will give you salvation.

But I must hasten on to the next class—the unsaved. I will admit that professed Christians have got their failings; we are far from being what we ought to be. But is that any reason why you should not come to Him? We do not preach ourselves, we do not set ourselves up as the Saviour; if we did you might make this an excuse. But we preach Christ. Now, you who are unsaved, won't you come? I do not know who you are in this audience, but if the Spirit of God is not born in you, and does not tell you that you are the children of God, this is an evidence that you have not been born of God. Do you love your enemies? Do you love those who slander you? Do you love those who hate you? Have you joy, peace, long-suffering, courage, charity? If you have got the fruit of the Spirit, you have those qualities; if you have not, you have not been born of the Spirit. Now, friends, just ask yourself this question, "Where am I?" Here I am in this hall to-day, surrounded with praying friends. It seemed sometimes to me as if the words came to me and fell to the floor; and at other times the words fell on the heart. We can feel it in this hall to-day in the atmosphere; we feel its influence all around. It may be that that mother is praying for the return of an erring son; it may be that that brother has been praying all the afternoon, "Oh, my God, may the Spirit come to my brother!" Dear friends, let us ask each other to-day, "Where art thou?" Resisting earnest, trembling prayers of some loving mother, of some loving wife—trampling them under-foot? Now, be honest. Have I not been talking to many in this audience who made promises five, ten, fifteen, twenty years ago—who made a promise to serve Him? Those promises have faded away, and those five, ten, twenty years have rolled on and you are no nearer. Oh, sinner, where art thou? Are you making light of all offers of mercy? Are you turning your back and ridiculing Him and laughing at Him?

If you are, may He, the God of mercy, arrest you and have mercy on your soul and save you. The last three years have been the most solemn years of my life. A man's life is just like going up and down a hill. If I live the allotted time, I am going down the hill. Many of you are on the top of the hill and are not saved. Suppose you pause a moment and look down the hill on the road from whence you came—look back toward the cradle. Don't you remember that the sermons you heard ten or fifteen years ago moved you? You say, when you look back at those times, "We used to have good sermons, better and more earnest ministers than now." Don't you make any mistake. The Gospel is the same as it was then, as powerful to-day as ever. The fault is not with the ministers or the Gospel; it is with yourself; your heart has become hard. Then, as you look down into the valley, don't you see a little mound and a tombstone? It marks the resting-place of a loving father, or a loving mother. Ten years ago you had a praying mother. Every morning and evening she went down on her knees in her closet and prayed for you. Her prayers are ended now, and yet you are not saved. It may be, as you look down the stream of time, you see a little grave that marks the resting-place of your child. It may be that child took you by the hand, and asked you, "Will you meet me in that land?" And you promised her that you would meet her there. As you looked down into that little grave and heard the damp, cold earth falling down, you repeated that promise. Five, ten, fifteen years ago you promised this; have you kept it? Some of you are far down the hill and hastening to judgment. May God open your eyes to-day as you look back upon your lives and look into the future. It may be that you will live the allotted time, but the end is soon to come. The average age is thirty-three years. There are a number of you in this hall this afternoon who will be in eternity inside of thirty days. Ask yourselves where you are; resisting the offer of mercy, turning back the offer of God. May the loving God show you the Saviour standing at the door of your heart, and knocking and telling you He wants to come in and save you.

In London, when I was there in 1867, I was told a story which made a very deep impression upon me. A young French noble-

man came there to see a doctor, bringing letters from the French
Emperor. The Emperor Napoleon III had a great regard for
this young man, and the doctor wanted to save him. He examined
the young man, and saw there was something upon his mind.
"Have you lost any property? What is troubling you? You have
something weighing upon your mind," said the doctor. "Oh,
there is nothing particular." "I know better; have you lost any
relations?" asked the doctor. "No, none within the last three
years." "Have you lost any reputation in your country?" "No."
The doctor studied for a few minutes, and then said, "I must
know what is on your mind; I must know what is troubling
you." And the young man said, "My father was an infidel; my
grandfather was an infidel, and I was brought up an infidel, and
for the last three years these words have haunted me, 'Eternity,
and where shall it find me?'" "Ah," said the doctor, "you have
come to the wrong physician." "Is there no hope for me?" cried
the young man. "I walk about in the daytime; I lie down at
night, and it comes upon me continually; 'Eternity, and where
shall I spend it?' Tell me, is there any hope for me?" The
doctor said: "Now just sit down and be quiet. A few years ago
I was an infidel. I did not believe in God, and was in the same
condition in which you are." The doctor took down his Bible
and turned to the fifty-third chapter of Isaiah and read: "He was
wounded for our transgressions, he was bruised for our iniquities:
the chastisement of our peace was upon him; and with his stripes
we are healed." And he read on through this chapter. When he
had finished, the young man said: "Do you believe this, that He
voluntarily left Heaven, came down to this earth, and suffered
and died that we might be saved?" "Yes, I believe it. That
brought me out of infidelity, out of darkness into light." And he
preached Christ and His salvation and told him of Heaven, and
then suggested that they get down on their knees and pray. And
when I went there in 1876 a letter had been received from that
young nobleman, who wrote to Dr. Whinston in London, telling
him that question of "eternity, and where he should spend it,"
was settled and troubled him no more. My friends, this question
of eternity, and where we are going to spend it, forces itself upon
every one of us. We are staying here for a little day. Our life

is but a fibre, and it will soon be snapped. I may be preaching my last sermon. To-night may find me in eternity. By the grace of God say that you will spend it in Heaven. All the hosts of hell cannot hinder you if you make up your mind to come to Heaven, because if God says, "Let him come," who can resist you? If that little child sitting yonder says it will enter Heaven, all the hosts of hell cannot keep it out. May God help you to spend your eternity in Heaven, and may you say: "By the grace of God I accept Jesus as my Redeemer."

"THEIR ROCK IS NOT AS OUR ROCK"

DEUTERONOMY 32:31

Preface

THIS REMARKABLE SERMON, considering that the text itself is not one of the best known in the Scriptures, was preached again and again by Mr. Moody over a quarter of a century. Sometimes it was entitled "The Religion of Jesus Better than all Isms." This is the only printed sermon by Mr. Moody known to me in which he spends no little time in informing his audience regarding the definitions from Webster's Dictionary of such words as *deist, pantheist* and *infidel*. We have here twenty-three illustrations, some brief and some long, which total ten pages of the fourteen devoted to this one sermon. Here Mr. Moody introduced a factor in his preaching which is seldom to be found in his printed sermons, that is, extensive quotations from letters which he had received. He here uses the famous illustration of the writings of Lord Lyttleton and Gilbert West on the conversion of St. Paul and the resurrection of Christ. It would be interesting to know where Mr. Moody acquired his illustration from the life of Sir Isaac Newton.

The remarkable consequences of this sermon in London to a great gathering of infidels is to be found in the Introduction to this volume. The sermon here printed is to be found in *Great Joy*, pp. 370-83. It is also in *Great Redemption* (1889), pp. 135-51; *Sermons, Addresses, and Prayers* (1877), pp. 445-54; and *Gospel Awakening* (1879), pp. 492-501.

"Their Rock Is Not as Our Rock"

I WANT TO CALL YOUR ATTENTION to-night to a text which you will find in the thirty-second chapter of Deuteronomy and thirty-first verse: "For their rock is not as our Rock, even our enemies themselves being judges." I wish that this audience for about thirty minutes would just imagine they are sitting in judgment—that each one is sitting upon the case brought up. We want every man, woman and child in this building to decide the question brought before them. "For their rock is not as our Rock, even our enemies themselves being judges." This was uttered by Moses in his farewell address to Israel. He had been with them forty years, day and night. He had been the king, or president, or judge, or whatever you may call it; he had been their leader or instructor, in other words he had been a god to them, for all the blessings of heaven came through him. And the old man was about leaving them. He had taken them to the borders of the promised land, and all who had left Egypt with him, but Joshua and Caleb, had been laid in that wilderness. Now he is making his farewell address; and, young man, if you have never read it, read it to-night. It is the best sermon in print. I do not know any other sermon in the New or Old Testament that compares with it. His natural activity hadn't abated—he had still the vigor of youth. I can see him as he delivers it: his long white hair flowing over his shoulders, and his venerable beard covering his breast as he gives them the wholesome instruction. Now, I want every one to wake up here. I see one young man over there who has just gone to sleep. All you young men will help me if you see anyone next you going to sleep by pinching his elbow. We don't want any one here to sleep. I remember when I was in Boston I fell asleep in church, and a man just pinched me and I rubbed my eyes and woke up. I looked at the minister, and lo and behold, I thought he was preaching directly at me. It seemed as if he knew all about my faults, and my disposition, and everything about me. I never felt so cheap in my life. All his remarks seemed to be directed to me, and I wondered who had been telling that minister about me. At the

conclusion of the sermon I pulled my coat-collar up and got out
as quick as I could. Now, bear in mind, you men who have gone
to sleep are the very men I want to speak to. But let us go back
to the subject. The old man was giving his farewell address,
in which he said, "This rock is not as our Rock, even our enemies
themselves being judges." Now I am not going to call upon
Christians to settle this question, but the ungodly, the unconverted, must decide this question, and if you be fair with the
argument you will have to admit that "Your rock is not as our
rock"; your peace is not as our peace; because we have got our
feet on the rock of Jesus.

You know, in the first place, that the atheist does not believe
in any God. He denies the existence of a God. Now, I contend
that his rock is not as our rock, and will let those atheists be
the judges. What does an atheist look forward to? Nothing.
He is taking a very crooked path in this world. His life has been
dark; it has been full of disappointments. When he was a young
man ambition beckoned him on to a certain height. He has attained to that height, but he is not satisfied. He climbs a little
higher, and perhaps he has got as far as he can get, but he is not
contented. He is dissatisfied, and if he takes a look into the
future he sees nothing. Man's life is full of trouble. Afflictions
are as numerous as the hairs of our head, but when the billows
of affliction are rising and rolling over him he has no God to
call upon, therefore, I contend his "rock is not as our Rock."
Look at him. He has a child. That atheist has all the natural
affection for that child possible. He has a son—a noble young
man—who starts out in life full of promise, but he goes astray.
He has not the will-power of his father, and cannot resist the
temptation of the world. That father cannot call upon God to
save his son. He sees that son go down to ruin step by step, and
by-and-by he plunges into a hopeless, godless, Christless grave.
And as that father looks into that grave he has no hope. His
"rock is not as our Rock." Look at him again. He has a child
laid low with fever, racked with pain and torture, but the poor
atheist cannot offer any consolation to that child. As he stands
by the bedside of that child she says, "Father, I am dying; in a
little while I will go into another world. What is going to be-

come of me? Am I going to die like a dumb beast?" "Yes," the poor atheist says, "I love you, my daughter; but you will soon be in the grave and eaten up with the worms, and that will be all. There is no heaven, no hereafter; it is all a myth. People have been telling you there is a hereafter, but they have been deluding you." Did you ever hear an atheist going to his dying children and telling them this? My friends, when the hour of affliction comes they call in a minister to give consolation. Why don't the atheists preach no hereafter, no heaven, no God, in the hour of affliction? This very fact is an admission that "their rock is not as our Rock, even our enemies themselves being the judges." But look again. That little child dies, and that atheist father follows the body to the grave and lays it down in its resting place and says: "All that is left of my child is there; it will soon become the companion of worms, who will feed upon it. That is all there is." Why, the poor man's heart is broken, and he will admit his "rock is not as our Rock." A prominent atheist went to the grave with the body of his friend. He pronounced a eulogy, and committed all that was left of his friend to the winds—to nature— and bade the remains farewell forever. Oh, my friends, had he any consolation then? His rock was not as our rock.

A good many years ago there was a convention held in France, and those who held it wanted to get the country to deny a God, to burn the Bible, wanted to say that a man passed away like a dog—like a dumb animal. What was the result? Not long after, that country was filled with blood. Did you ever think what would take place if we could vote the Bible and the ministers of the gospel and God out from among the people? My friends, the country would be deluged with blood. Your life and mine would not be safe in this city to-night. We could not walk through those streets with safety. We don't know how much we owe God and the influence of His gospel among even ungodly men. I can imagine some of you saying, "Why this talk about atheists? There are none here." Well, I hope there isn't; but I find a great number who come into the inquiry-rooms—just to look on, who confess they don't believe in any God or any hereafter.

But there is another class called deists, who, you know, don't believe in revelation—who don't believe in Jesus Christ. Ask a deist who is his God. "Well," he will say, "He is the beginning— He who caused all things." These deists say there is no use to pray, because nothing can change the decrees of their deity; God never answers prayer. "Their rock is not as our Rock." In the hour of affliction they, too, send off for some Christian to administer consolation. But there is another class. They say, "I am no deist; I am a pantheist; I believe that God is in the air; He is in the sun, the stars, in the rain, in the water"—they say God is in this wood. Why, a pantheist the other night told me God was in that post; he was in the floor. When we come to talk to those pantheists, we find them no better than the deists and atheists. There was one of that sort that Sir Isaac Newton went to talk to. He used to argue with him, and try to get the pantheist into his belief, but he couldn't. In the hour of his distress, however, he cried out to the God of Sir Isaac Newton. Why don't they cry to their God in the hour of their trouble? When I used to be in this city I used to be called on to attend a good many funerals. I would inquire what the man was in his belief. If I found out he was an atheist or a deist, or a pantheist, when I would go to the funeral and, in the presence of his friends said one word about that man's doctrine, they would feel insulted. Why is it that, in a trying hour, when they have been talking all the time against God—why is it that in the darkness of affliction they call in believers in that God to administer consolation?

The next class I want to call attention to is the infidel. I contend his "rock" is not as our "rock." Look at an infidel. An infidel is one who don't believe in the inspiration of Scripture. These men are very numerous, and they feel insulted when we call them infidels; but the man who don't believe in the inspiration of Scripture is an infidel. A good many of them are in the church, and not a few of them have crept into the pulpit. These men would feel insulted if we called them infidels, but if a man says—I don't care who he is or where he preaches—if he tries to say that the Bible is not inspired from back to back he is an infidel. That is their true name, although they don't like to be called that. Now in that blessed book there are five hundred or six hundred prophecies, and every one of them has been fulfilled to the letter; and yet men say they cannot believe the Bible is inspired. As I said the other night, those who cannot believe it have never read it. I hear a great many infidels talk against the Bible, but I haven't found the first man who ever read the Bible from back to back carefully and remained an infidel. My friends, the Bible of our mothers and fathers is true. How many men have said to me, "Mr. Moody, I would give the world if I had your faith, your consolation, the hope you have from your religion." Is not that a proof that "their rock is not as our Rock"? Now look at these prophecies in regard to Nineveh, in regard to Babylon, to Egypt, to the Jewish nation, and see how literally they have been fulfilled to the letter. Every promise God makes He carries out. But although infidels prefer their disbelief in the inspiration of Scripture, they do not believe in their hearts what they declare, else why, when we talk with them, if they have any children, do they send them out of the room? Now, not long ago, I went into a man's house, and when I commenced to talk about religion he turned to his daughter and said, "You had better go out of the room; I want to say a few words to Mr. Moody." When she had gone he opened a perfect torrent of infidelity upon me. "Why," said I, "did you send your daughter out of the room before you said this?" "Well," he replied, "I did not think it would do her any good to hear what I said." My friends, his "rock is not as our Rock." Why did he send his daughter out of the room if he believed what he said? It was because he did not believe it. Why, if I believed in infidelity I would wish my daughters and my sons, my wife, and all belonging to me sharers in the same belief. I would preach it wherever I went. But they doubt what they advocate. If they believed it down in their souls why, when their daughters die, do they send for a true Christian to administer consolation? Why don't they send for some follower of Voltaire, or Hume, or Paine? Why, when they make their last will, do they send for some Christian to carry it out? My friends, it is because their rock has no foundation; it is because in the hour of adversity, in spite of all their boasts of the grandeur of infidelity, they cannot trust

their infidel friends. "Their rock is not as our Rock, even our
enemies themselves being judges."

Now, did you ever hear of a Christian in his dying hour re-
canting? You never did. Did you ever hear of Christians regret-
ting that they had accepted Christianity, and in their dying hour
embracing infidelity? I would like to see the man who could
stand and say he had. But how many times have Christians been
called to the bedside of an atheist, or deist, or infidel in his
dying hours, and heard him crying for mercy? In that hour infidelity is gone, and he wants the God of his father and mother
to take the place of his black infidelity. It is said of West, an
eminent man, that he was going to take up the doctrine of the
resurrection, and show the world what a fraud it-was, while Lord
Lyttleton was going to take up the conversion of Saul, and just
show the folly of it. These men were going to annihilate that
doctrine and that incident of the gospel. They were going to
emulate the Frenchman, who said it took twelve fishermen to
build up Christ's religion, but one Frenchman pulled it down.
From Calvary this doctrine rolled along the stream of time,
through the eighteen hundred years, down to us, and West got
at it and began to look at the evidence; but instead of being
able to cope with it he found it perfectly overwhelming—the
proof that Christ had risen, that He had come out of the sepulcher, and ascended to heaven and led captivity captive. The
light dawned upon him, and he became an expounder of the
word of God and a champion of Christianity. And Lord Lyttleton, that infidel and skeptic, hadn't been long at the conversion
of Saul before the God of Saul broke upon his sight and he too
began to preach. I don't believe there is a man in the audience
who, if he will take his Bible and read it, but will be convinced
of its truth. What does infidelity do for a man? "Why," said a
dying infidel, "my principles have lost me my friends; my principles have sent my wife to her grave with a broken heart; they
have made my children beggars, and I go down to my grave
without peace or consolation." I never heard of an infidel going
down to his grave happily. But not only do they go on without
peace, but how many youths do they turn away from God? How

many young men are turned away from Christ by these infidels and devils? Let them remember that God will hold them responsible if they are guilty of turning men away from heaven. A few infidels gathered around a dying friend lately, and they wanted him to hold on to the end, to die like a man. They were trying to cheer him, but the poor infidel turned to them. "Ah," said he, "what have I got to hold on to?" My friends, let me ask you what you have got to hold on to? Every Christian has Christ to hold on to—the resurrected man. "I am he that liveth, and was dead; and, behold, I am alive for evermore." Thank God, we have some one to carry us through all our trials. But what has the infidel got to hold on to; what hope has the atheist, deist, or pantheist? His gods are false gods.

They are like the false gods of the Hebrews; they never hear their cry. Whereas, if we have the God of Daniel, of Abraham, He is always ready to succor us when in distress, and we can make Him our fortress, and we have a refuge in the storm of adversity. There we can anchor safely, free from danger and disaster. I was reading to-night almost the last words of Lord Byron, and I want to draw a comparison between the sorrowful words of Byron and those of Saint Paul. He died very young— he was only thirty-six—after leading an ungodly life.

> My days are in the yellow leaf,
>   The flower and fruit of life are gone;
> The worm, the canker and the grief
>   Are mine alone.

Compare those words with the words of St. Paul. "I have fought a good fight, I have finished my course, I have kept the faith. Henceforth there is laid up for me a crown of righteousness, which the Lord, the righteous judge, shall give me at that day." What a contrast! What a difference! My friends, there is as much difference between them as there is between heaven and hell, between death and life. Be judges of which is the most glorious—atheism, deism, infidelity, or the Christianity of St. Paul. May God take all these isms and sweep them from the world.

I want to read to you a letter which I received some time ago.

I read this to you because I am getting letters from infidels who say that not an infidel has repented during our meetings. Only about ten days ago I got a letter from an infidel, who accused me of being a liar. He said there had not been an infidel converted during our meetings. My friends, go up to the young converts' meeting any Monday night, and you will see there ten or twelve every night who have accepted Christ. Why, nearly every night we meet with a poor infidel who accepts Christ. But let me read this letter. We get many letters every day for prayer, and, my friends, you don't know the stories that lie behind those letters. The letter I am about to read was not received here, but while we were in Philadelphia. When I received it I put it away, intending to use it at a future day:

"Dear Sir: Allow me the privilege of addressing you with a few words. The cause of writing is indeed a serious one. I am the son of an aristocratic family of Germany—was expensively educated, and at college at Leipsic was ruined by drinking, etc.; was expelled for gambling and dishonesty. My parents were greatly grieved at my conduct, and I did not dare return home, but sailed for America. I went to St. Louis, and remained there for want of money to get away. I finally obtained a situation as bookkeeper in a dry goods house; heard from home and the death of my parents. This made me more sinful than ever before. I heard one of your sermons, which made a deep impression on me. I was taken sick, and the words of your text came to me and troubled me. I have tried to find peace of God, but have not succeeded. My friends, by reasoning with me that there was no God, endeavored to comfort me. The thought of my sinfulness and approaching the grave, my blasphemy, my bad example, caused me to mourn and weep. I think God is too just to forgive me my sins. My life is drawing to a close. I have not yet received God's favor. Will you not remember me in your prayer, and beseech God to save my soul from eternal destruction? Excuse me for writing this, but it will be the last I shall write this side of the grave."

Ah, my friends, his "rock was not as our Rock," even our enemies themselves being judges. I have two more letters I would like to read. I am not accustomed to read so many letters, but on this occasion I will read them to you. Some of you remember me speaking of a man who came in here who was a fugitive from justice. The Governor of the State from which he came had offered a reward for him, and he came into this Tabernacle. He received Christ, and returned to his State. This morning I received the following letter:

"Dear Sir and Brother: Owing to the law's slow delay I am yet a prisoner of hope. By Thursday or Friday my case will be reached, and I'll be committed to the Penitentiary, how long I do not know. This condition is voluntary, or of my own seeking, because I feel it due the cause of God, or the only evidence I can give of my repentance and desire to do better. My family and friends hope ultimately to obtain a pardon. I desire to thank you for the interest you have taken in me, and I ask your prayers, and those of God's people in Chicago, that I may have strength and grace to live under these calamities, that my poor heartbroken wife and children may be sustained, and, further, that God's blessing may rest on all efforts being made for my future. After it is all over, and I am in a felon's cell, I'll write you. In your efforts to warn men to do better and lead a new life, bid them beware of ambition to accomplish an undertaking at all hazards. Such is my condition. Had I left off speculation in an invention I might now be happy. Step by step I yielded until my forgeries reached over $30,000. My aim was not to defraud, but to succeed, and pay it all back. Oh, pray for me—for all who suffer with me. While in Chicago I was under an assumed name. Here I am, in my native village, in my father's home, a prisoner, not daring to go out, or even to see my children (we have three, two boys and one girl). I hear their voices, and when they sleep, I silently go in their little room and look at them in their innocent slumber. My crimes are in another county, whither I go Thursday. May our heavenly Father bless your labors. Humbly and repentant I am."

To-morrow probably he will go into the penitentiary to suffer for his crime, but now his rock is our rock.

Last week a beautiful-looking young man came into the inquiry room. He had been brought up in a happy home with a good father and mother. He had gone astray. When he came into the inquiry room he said he intended to become a Christian, but he could not because he knew what it would make him do. He had robbed an express company and that sin came between him and God. He had been heard and received a verdict in his favor, but he knew he was guilty. He had gone into the witness box and committed perjury. He turned away and left the building. Last Friday, however, he was at the noonday meeting; he was in my private room for a while, and I never felt so much pity for a man in my life. He wanted to become a Christian, but he thought of having to go back and tell his father that he was guilty, after his father had paid $2,000 to conduct his trial. After a great struggle he got down on his knees and cried out, "O God, help me; forgive me my sins"; and at last he got up and straightened himself and said, "Well, sir, I will go back." A friend went down to the railway station and saw him off, and shortly after I got this dispatch from him:

"Mr. Moody—God has told me what to do. The future is as clear as crystal. I am happier than ever before."

He went on his way, reaching his native village, and I received this letter from him this morning, and I have felt my soul filled with sorrow ever since it came. Let me say here, if there is anyone in this hall who has taken money from his employer, go and tell him of it at once. It is a good deal better for you to confess it than have it on your mind—than to try to cover it up. "He that covereth his sins shall not prosper." If you have taken any money that don't belong to you, make restitution by confession at least. If any one here is being tempted to commit a forgery or any crime, let this be a warning to them:

"My Beloved Friend and Brother: I am firm in the cause. I have started, and feel that God is with me in it. And, oh, dear brother, do never cease praying for my dear father and praying mother, and I wish you would some day write them and tell them that God will make this all for the best. If I live for ages I will never cease praying for them, and I never can forgive myself for my ungratefulness to my dear broken-hearted sisters and brothers and dear good parents. Oh, that link that held the once happy home is severed. O God! may it not be forever. Would that I had been a Christian for life; that I had taken my mother's hand when a child and walked from there, hand in hand, straight to heaven; and then the stains would not have been. But we know, O God, that they can't follow me into heaven, for then I will be washed of all my sins, and the things that are on this earth will stay here.

"Oh, my dear Christian brothers, my heart almost failed me when I was approaching my dear, happy home, and the thought that I was the one out of eight brothers and sisters to break the chain of happiness that surround that once happy and beautiful home, which is now shaded with misery, and the beautiful sunshine that once lit that happy, that dearest of homes, is now overshadowed with darkness. Oh, I fear it will take my dear parents; it is more than they can bear. When I reached home, and they all greeted me with a kiss, and I told them I had started for heaven, and God sent me home to tell them, my mother shed tears of happiness, and when I was forced to bring the death-stroke upon her the tears ceased to flow, and God only can describe the scene that took place. I called them all around me, and I thought I could not pray if I were to attempt it. But when I knelt with them in prayer God just told me what to say, and I found it the will of God; and after I had prayed I kissed them all, and asked their pardon for my ungratefulness, which I received from them all. Then I made my preparation to leave home, for how long God only knows, but I got grace to leave in a cheerful way, and it appeared for a short time; and if God lets me live to return home I will join my mother's side, take her to church, and bring my brothers and sisters and father to God. We will all go to heaven together. My beloved brother, I must see you some day, and just tell you what God has done for me, and I know He will never forsake me, when I am shut up in those prison walls receiving the punishment I justly deserve for my crime. When I can't communicate with any one else I know I will not be shut off from God. Oh, glory!

"I came to Cleveland last night, and was going to get that money and return it to the General Superintendent, but my attorney had made that arrangement already. I find there is an indictment at Akron against me now for perjury, and I am going to take the morning train and go to Akron. Court is in progress now, and I am going to ask the court if there is an indictment against me, and if there is I will hear it and then plead guilty. I will write you again soon, and give you all the particulars and the length of my sentence."

I want to urge this letter upon your consideration as a warning. Think of the punishment that young man has brought upon himself; think of the agony of that father and mother when he broke the news to them—when he told them of his guilt. His "rock was not as our Rock." May God bless every young man here to-night, and may they be brought to the acceptation of salvation. May they turn to Thee, God of their fathers, and of their mothers, so that they can say, "Your rock is our rock—we are servants of God."

THE BLOOD OF THE NEW
TESTAMENT

MATTHEW 26:28

Preface

ONE OF THE THREE THEMES most frequently dwelt upon by Mr. Moody in his quarter of a century of preaching was the blood of Christ. Sometimes he would simply call the sermon "The Blood." Sometimes he would preach on "The Blood of the Old Testament" and other times on "The Blood of the New Testament." Occasionally this subject would be dealt with in his sermon on "The Scarlet Thread." There are eleven illustrations in the text of this sermon, which is in *Sermons, Addresses, and Prayers,* pp. 156-64, all of them short.

I would not be a bit surprised if Mr. Moody, as everyone else, found it very difficult to obtain any illustration which could in any adequate way illuminate the great sacrifice of Christ on the cross. It just stands by itself.

This particular sermon is found also in *Gospel Awakening* (1879), pp. 255-64; and *Holding the Fort,* pp. 217-27; *London Discourses* (1875), pp. 176-88. His sermon on "The Blood of the Old Testament" is found in *Gospel Awakening,* pp. 247-55; *Great Joy,* pp. 94-117; *Holding the Fort,* pp. 207-16. All these sermons and others, appear in the volume bearing the title, *The Blood* (1875). It is in this sermon that Mr. Moody makes one of his rare references in preaching to that famous gospel preacher and scholar of Boston, Dr. Edward Norris Kirk, whose ministry had such a great influence on Mr. Moody in his younger days.

The Blood of the New Testament

MATTHEW 26:28: "For this is my blood of the new testament, which is shed for many for the remission of
sins."

I WANT TO TAKE UP SOME PASSAGES referring to the subject of the
Precious Blood in the New Testament. Soon after we came
back from Europe to this country, I received a letter from a
lady saying that she had looked forward to our coming back to
this country with a great deal of interest, and that her interest
remained after we had commenced our services until I came
to the lecture on the blood, when she gave up all hope of our
doing any good. In closing that letter she said: "Where did
Jesus ever teach the perilous and barbarous doctrine that men
were to be redeemed by the shedding of His blood? Never!
Never did Jesus teach that monstrous idea." Let us turn to the
fourteenth chapter of Mark, twenty-fourth verse, and we will
find: "And he said unto them, This is my blood of the new testament, which is shed for many"; and also in Matthew 26:28: "For
this is my blood of the new testament, which is shed for many
for the remission of sins." There are a good many passages, but
it is not necessary to refer to more. If Christ did not teach it,
and also the Apostles—if Christ did not preach it, then I have
read my Bible, all these years, wrong. I haven't got the key to
the Scriptures; it is a sealed book to me, and if I don't preach
it—if I give it up, I've nothing left to preach. Take the blessed
doctrine of the blood out of my Bible and my capital is gone,
and I've got to take to something else.

I remember when in the old country a young man came to
me—a minister came around to me, and said he wanted to talk
with me. He said to me: "Mr. Moody, you are either all right
and I am all wrong, or else I am right and you are all wrong."
"Well, sir," said I, "you have the advantage of me. You have
heard me preach, and know what doctrines I hold, whereas I
have not heard you, and don't know what you preach." "Well,"
said he, "the difference between your preaching and mine is,
that you make out that salvation is got by Christ's death, and I

make out that it is attained by His life." "Now, what do you do with the passages bearing upon the death?" and I quoted the passages, "Without shedding of blood is no remission," and "He Himself bore our sins in His own body on the tree," and asked him what he did with them, for instance. "Never preach on them at all." I quoted a number of passages more, and he gave me the same answer. "Well, what do you preach?" I finally asked. "Moral essays," he replied. Said I, "Did you ever know anybody to be saved by that kind of thing—did you ever convert anybody by them?" "I never aimed at that kind of conversion; I mean to get men to Heaven by culture—by refinement." "Well," said I, "if I didn't preach those texts, and only preached culture, the whole thing would be a sham." "And it is a sham to me," was his reply. I tell you the moment a man breaks away from this doctrine of blood, religion becomes a sham, because the whole teaching of this book is of one story, and this is that Christ came into the world and died for our sins.

I want to call your attention to the nineteenth chapter of John and the thirty-fourth verse: "But one of the soldiers with a spear pierced his side, and forthwith came there out blood and water." "Came there out blood and water." Now, it was prophesied years before that there should open a fountain which should wash away sin and uncleanness, and it seems that this fountain was opened here by the spear of the soldier, and out of the fountain came blood and water. It was the breaking of the crown of hell and the giving of the crown to Heaven. When the Roman soldier drove out the blood, out came the water, and it touched that spear, and it was not long before Christ had that Roman government. It is a throne and a footstool now, and by and by it will sway the earth from pole to pole. This earth has been redeemed by the blessed blood of Christ. Peter says in his first Epistle 1:18: "Forasmuch as ye know that ye were not redeemed with corruptible things, as silver and gold, from your vain conversation received by tradition from your fathers; but with the precious blood of Christ, as of a lamb without blemish and without spot." You are not redeemed by such corruptible things as gold or silver, but by the precious blood of the Lamb—"the precious blood of Christ—as of a lamb without blemish." If silver and gold could have redeemed us, it would have been the easiest thing to have made a pile of gold ten thousand times larger than the bulk of the earth. Why, the poorest thing is gold in Heaven But gold couldn't do it. The law had been broken, and the penalty of death had come upon us, and it required life to redeem us. Now, it says we shall be redeemed. My friends, redemption is to me one of the most precious treasures in the Word of God—to think that Christ has bought me by His blood. I am no longer my own, I am His. He has ransomed me.

A friend of mine once told me that he was going out from Dublin one day, and met a boy who had one of those English sparrows in his hand. It was frightened, and just seemed to sit as if it pined for liberty, but the boy held it so tight that it could not get away. The boy's strength was too much for the bird. My friend said: "Open your hand and let the bird go. You will never tame him; he is wild." But the boy replied, "Faith, an' I'll not; I've been a whole hour trying to catch him, an' now I've got him I'm going to keep him." So the man took out his purse and asked the boy if he would sell it. A bargain was made, and the sparrow was transferred to the man's hand. He opened his hand, and at first the bird did not seem to realize it had liberty, but by and by it flew away, and as it went it chirped, as much as to say, "You have redeemed me." And so Christ has come down and offered to redeem us and give us liberty when we were bound with sin. Satan was stronger than we were. He has had six thousand years' experience. He did not come to buy us from Satan, but from the penalty of our sin.

Another thought about the blood. It makes us all one. The blood brings us into one family, into the household of faith. I remember during the war Dr. Kirk, one of the most eloquent men I ever heard, was speaking in Boston. At that time, you recollect, there was a good deal said about the Irish and the black man, and what an amount of talk about the war of races. He said while preaching one night: "I saw a poor Irishman and a black man and an Englishman, and the blood of Christ came down and fell upon them and made them one." My friends, it brings nationalities together; it brings those scattered with the seeds of discord together and makes them one. Let us turn to Acts 17:26, and we read: "And hath made of one blood all nations of men for to dwell on all the face of the earth, and hath determined the times before appointed, and the bounds of their habitation." That's what the blood of Christ does. It just makes us one. I can tell a man that has been redeemed by the blood; they speak all the same language. I don't require to be in his company ten minutes before I can tell whether or not he has been redeemed. They have only one language, and you can tell when they speak whether they are outside the blood or sheltered by it. The blood has two voices—one is for salvation and the other for condemnation. The blood to-night cries out for my salvation or for my condemnation. If we are sheltered behind the blood, it cries for our salvation, for we see in Galatians: "It cries for our peace." There is no peace till a man has been sheltered by that blood.

Again, I would like to call your attention to the twenty-sixth chapter of Matthew, twenty-eighth verse, where we find Christ speaking of His blood: "For this is my blood of the new testament, which is shed for the remission of sins." This blood was "shed for the remission of sins." Then in Hebrews ninth and twenty-second, where it says, "Without the shedding of blood is no remission of sins." Men don't realize that this is God's plan of salvation. Said a man to me last night after the meeting: "Why, God has got a plan to save us." Certainly He has. You must be saved by God's plan. It was love that prompted God to send His Son to save us and shed His blood. That was the plan. And without the blood what hope have you? There is not a sin from your childhood—from your cradle—up till now that can be forgiven, unless by the blood. Let us take God at His word: "Without the shedding of blood there is no remission of sins." Without the blood no remission whatever. I don't see how a man can fail to comprehend this. That's what Christ died for; that's what Christ died on Calvary for. If a man makes light of that blood what hope has he? How are you going to get into the kingdom of God? You cannot join in the song of the saints if you don't go into Heaven that way. You cannot sing the song of redemption. If you did, I suppose you would be off in some corner with a harp of your own, and singing, "I saved myself;

I saved myself." You can't get in that way. You must accept
the plan of redemption and come in through it. "He that
climbeth up some other way, the same is a thief and a robber."

Then, in the tenth chapter of Hebrews, we find Paul, if he
wrote this, just taking up the very thought: "He that despised
Moses' law died without mercy under two or three witnesses."
You know when a man made light of the law under the Mosaic
dispensation, whenever two witnesses came into court and swore
that he hadn't kept the law, they just took him out and stoned
him to death. Take up the next verse: "Of how much sorer
punishment suppose ye, shall he be thought worthy, who hath
trodden under foot the Son of God, and hath counted the blood
of the covenant, wherewith he was sanctified, an unholy thing,
and hath done despite unto the Spirit of grace." My friends, what
hope is there if a man tramples the blood of Christ under his
foot, if he says, "I will have nothing to do with that blood?" I
ask, in all candor, what mercy is there? What hope has he if he
"hath trodden under foot the Son of God, and hath counted
the blood of the covenant, wherewith he was sanctified, an unholy thing"? This is the only way to get to Heaven—no other
way. Turn again to the eleventh verse of the same chapter, and
we see: "But this man, after he had offered one sacrifice for
sins"—mark that, He had settled the question of sin—"for ever
sat down on the right hand of God." The high-priests could never
sit down; their work was never done. But our High-Priest had
put sin away by one sacrifice and then ascended to God. And in
this same chapter of Hebrews we see again: "Having therefore,
brethren, boldness to enter into the holiest by the blood of Jesus,
by a new and living way, which he hath consecrated for us,
through the veil, that is to say, his flesh; and having an high
priest over the house of God; let us draw near with a true heart
in full assurance of faith, having our hearts sprinkled from an evil
conscience, and our bodies washed with pure water. Let us hold
fast the profession of our faith without wavering; for he is faithful
that promised." I want to call your attention to the twentieth
verse more particularly—"by a new and living way." Now Christ
has opened a new and living way. We cannot get to heaven by
our own deeds now. He has opened "a new and living way."

We don't need a high-priest to go once a year and pray to God. Thank God, we are all kings and high-priests. We can go right straight to the Father in the name of the Lord Jesus Christ. When Christ died that veil was rent from the top to the bottom—not from the bottom to the top—and every poor son of Adam can walk right in and worship—right into the presence of God, if he only comes by the way of the blood. Yes, thank God, He has opened a new and living way whereby we can come to Him. Let us thank Him for a new and living way. We don't need any bishop, we don't need any pope, we don't need any priest or prophet now; but every one can be made king and priest and we can come through this living way to His presence and ask Him to take away our sins. There's not a man in this assemblage but can come to Him to-night.

There's a good deal about the blood in Hebrews that I would like to bring up; time passes, and I have just to fly through the subject. Now I don't know any doctrine I have preached that has been talked about more than the doctrine of blood. Why, the moment Satan gets a man to leave out this doctrine of blood, he has gained all he wants. It is the most pernicious idea to leave it out. A man may be a brilliant preacher, he may have a brilliant intellect, and may have large crowds of people; but if he leaves this out, no one will be blest under his ministry, no one will be born in God's kingdom. If a man leaves out this blood he may as well go and whistle in the streets, and try to convert people that way, for all the good he will do in saving souls. It is said that old Dr. Alexander, of Princeton College, when a young student used to start out to preach always gave them a piece of advice. The old man would stand with his gray locks and his venerable face and say, "Young man, make much of the blood in your ministry." Now, I have traveled considerably during the past few years, and never met a minister who made much of the blood and much of the atonement, but God had blessed his ministry, and souls were born into the light by it. But a man who leaves it out—the moment he goes, his church falls to pieces like a rope of sand, and his preaching has been barren of good results. And so if you find a man preaching who has covered up this doctrine of blood, don't sit under his ministry; I don't care what denomination he belongs to, get out of it. Fly from it as those who flew from Sodom. Never mind how you get out of it—leave it. It is a whited sepulcher. There is no life if they don't preach the blood. It is the only way we've got to conquer Satan—the only way we can enter Heaven, and we cannot get there unless we have washed our robes in the blood of the Lamb. If we expect to conquer, we must first be washed by that blood. A man who has not realized what the blood has done for him, has not the token of salvation. It is told of Julian, the apostate, that while he was fighting, he received an arrow in his side. He pulled it out, and taking a handful of blood, threw it into the air, and cried, "Galilean, Galilean, thou hast conquered!" Yes, the Galilean is going to conquer, and you must bear in mind if you don't accept the blood—don't submit to it and let it cleanse you—the rock will fall on you, because the decree of Heaven is that every knee shall bow to the will of Heaven. The blood is a call of mercy now. He wants you to come—He beseeches you to accept and be saved.

I heard of an old minister who had preached the Gospel for fifty years faithfully. "Ah!" many here will say, "I wish I was as safe to go to Heaven as him." When he was reaching his end he asked that his Bible should be brought to him. His eyes were growing dim in death, and he said to one of those about him, "I wish you would turn to the first epistle of John 1:7," and when it was found, the old man put his dying finger on the passage where it says: "But if we walk in the light, as he is in the light, we have fellowship one with another, and the blood of Jesus Christ his Son cleanseth us from all sin," and he said, "I die in the hope of that." It was the blood in his ministry that cleansed him. And so it is the only way by which our sins can be washed away. Why, there was a question once asked in Heaven when a great crowd were gathering there, "Who are those?" and the answer was, "They are those who have come up through great tribulation, and have been washed by the blood of the Lamb."

Now, the question is, what are you going to do with that blood? I would like to ask you, what are you going to do about it? You must do either of two things—take it or reject it. Trample it under foot or cleanse your sins by it. I heard of a lady who told a servant to cook a lamb. She told him how to do it up and all about it, but she didn't tell him what to do with the blood. So he went to her and asked, "What are you going to do with the blood of the lamb?" She had been under conviction for some time, and such a question went like an arrow to her soul. She went to her room and felt uneasy, and the question kept continually coming to her, "What are you going to do with the blood of the lamb?" and before morning she was on her knees asking for the mercy of the blood of the Lamb.

Now the most solemn truth in the Gospel is that the only thing He left down here is His blood. His body and bones He took away, but He left His blood on Calvary. There is either of two things we must do. One is to send back the message to Heaven that we don't want the blood of Christ to cleanse us of our sin, or else accept it. Why, when we come to our dying hour the blood will be worth more than all the kingdoms of the world to us. Can you afford to turn your back upon it and make light of it? Dr. King, when the war was going on, went down to the field with the Christian Commission. He used to go around among the soldiers, and during one of his visits he heard a man cry, "Blood! Blood! Blood!" He thought that, as the man had just been taken off the battlefield, the scene of carnage and blood was still upon his mind. The doctor went to him and tried to talk to the man about Christ, and tried to divert his mind from the scenes of the field. "Ah, doctor," said the man feebly, "I was not thinking of the battle-field, but of the blood of Christ"; and he whispered the word "blood" once more and was gone.

Dear friends, do you want all your sins washed away from you? It was shed for the remission of sins, and without the shedding of blood there would be no remission. There is blood on the mercy-seat. "I am not looking to your sins now," God says, "but come and press in, press in and receive remission." Thank God, the blood is still on the mercy-seat. It is there, and He beseeches you to accept it. What more can He do for your salvation? Now, my friends, don't go out of this Tabernacle laughing and scoffing at the precious offering made to you, but just bow your head and lift up your voice, "Oh, God of Heaven, may the blood of Thy Son cleanse me from all sin." The blood is sufficient.

Some years ago I was journeying to the Pacific coast, and nearly every stage-driver I met was talking about a prominent stage-driver who had just died. You know that in driving over those rocky roads they depend a good deal upon the brake. This poor man, when he was dying, was heard to say: "I am on the down grade and cannot keep the brake." Just about that time one of the most faithful men of God, Alfred Cookman, passed away. His wife and friends gathered around his death-bed, and when his last moments arrived, it seemed as if Heaven had opened before him, as with a shout he cried, "I am sweeping through the gates washed by the blood of the Lamb." What a comfort this must have been to his friends; what a comfort it must have been to him, the blood of the atonement in his last hours.

My friends, if you want a glorious end like the end of that sainted man, you must come to the blood of Christ. Let us bow our heads in prayer; let us have a few moments of silent prayer, and let us ask the Lord to let us see this great truth.

Mr. Sankey sang the following hymn, as a song-translation of the story told by Mr. Moody, at the conclusion of his sermon:

> I am now a child of God,
>   For I'm washed in Jesus' blood;
> I am watching, and I'm longing while I wait.
>   Soon on wings of love I'll fly
>   To my home beyond the sky,
> To my welcome, as I'm sweeping thro' the gate.
>
> Refrain—In the blood of yonder Lamb,
>   Washed from every stain I am;
> Robed in whiteness, clad in brightness,
>   I am sweeping thro' the gates.
>
>   Oh! the blessed Lord of light,
>   I loved Him with my might;
> Now His arms enfold and comfort while I wait.
>   I am leaning on His breast,
>   Oh! the sweetness of His rest.
> And I'm thinking of my sweeping thro' the gate.

Burst are all my prison bars,
And I soar beyond the stars;
To my Father's house, the bright and blest estate.
Lo! the morn eternal breaks
And the song immortal wakes,
Robed in whiteness, I am sweeping thro' the gate.

THE "I WILLS" OF CHRIST

Preface

NOT A GREAT DEAL needs to be said about the contents of this sermon. The eight illustrations that are used are not unusual. Here is one of Mr. Moody's rare references in a sermon to a specific book. Inasmuch as all the references are not given in the sermon, perhaps readers would appreciate a complete list of those passages used by Mr. Moody in which our Lord expresses His own determination to do this or that. These references are Matthew 11:28; John 6:37; Luke 5:13; Matthew 10:32; 4:18; John 14:18 and Matthew 28:20 (without indicating it, Mr. Moody uses both of these texts for one point) ; John 4:40, 44, 54; and John 17:24.

This particular text is to be found in *The Faith Which Overcomes* (1884), pp. 107-124. This sermon also appeared in *Gospel Awakening* (1879) pp. 479-87; *Great Joy* (1879), pp. 340-51; *The Old Gospel and Other Addresses* (1882), pp. 81-90; *The Overcoming Life and Other Sermons* (1896), pp. 110-27; and *New Sermons, Addresses, and Prayers* (1877), pp. 429-37. The sermon was separately published in London in 1875.

The "I Wills" of Christ

I WANT TO CALL YOUR ATTENTION to-night to the eight "I wills" of
Christ. Now, when we say "I will" very often it don't mean much.
My friends, I want you to pay attention to the text. I see some
of you looking after Mr. Sankey. (Mr. Sankey moving out.)
You may forget the songs which have been sung to-night, you
may forget the sermon, but if the text gets down to your heart
you will never forget it. The eight "I wills" of Christ. I was
going to say that a man, when he says "I will," may not mean
much. We very often say "I will" when we don't mean to fulfil
what we say, but when we come to the "I will" of Christ, He
means to fulfil it; everything He has promised to do He is able
and willing to accomplish, and He is going to do it. I cannot
find any passage in Scripture in which He says "I will" do this,
or "I will" do that, but it will be done. The first "I will" I want
to call your attention to occurs in Matthew 11:28: "Come unto
me, all ye that labour, and are heavy laden, and I will give you
rest. Take my yoke upon you, and learn of me; for I am meek
and lowly in heart: and ye shall find rest unto your souls. For
my yoke is easy and my burden is light." Now, what is it that
man wants more than rest? What is it that the world is in pursuit
of? What are all the men in Chicago after if it isn't rest? What
do business men toil for if it isn't rest? Why do men spend their
lives in hunting for wealth if it is not for rest? But my friends,
that is not the way to get rest. A man cannot find it in wealth:
he cannot find it in pleasure. Take the pleasure-seekers of Chicago, and ask them if they have rest. They are like the waves of
the sea, perpetually troubled. My friends, the man who is away
from God never knows what rest is. You can see this in their
faces—in the wrinkles of their brow. They don't know what rest
is. What does Christ say: "Come unto me, all ye that labour, and
are heavy laden, and I will give you rest." It isn't in the market
for sale. How many men in Chicago would not gladly go up to
the Board of Trade to-morrow morning, and give thousands for
it if it was for sale? They would give thousands of dollars for it
if they could buy it. But it ain't for sale. If you get it you must
take it as a gift from Him who came from heaven to give it. The

moment a man is willing to take it as a gift it is his. There is one thing I notice: that a man goes in every direction, seeks every means, tries every person for rest before he comes to the true source. He will try to get rest in the world, he will try to find honor in pleasure, in politics, but he won't get it. You cannot find one of these politicians who knows what rest is; you cannot find one of those business men who knows what rest is unless he has Christ. Ask any man who is after the things of the world if he really knows what rest is, and he will answer you "no." If you come to Christ he tells you: "I will" give it. I like this "I will." He means it; and if you want rest, go to-night and say you are weary and your soul is seeking rest, and He will give it. He will give it without price. Take it. "O man, thou hast destroyed thyself, but in Me is thine help." In Him is your help and in Him will you find rest. If there is a poor, mangled one here, come to Christ to-night and confess to Him. Come to Christ and He will take your burden away and put it behind His back, and He will give that weary soul rest. Now, just test it to-night. Let every one who is weary and heavy-laden come to Him to-night.

The next "I will" is in John, sixth chapter: "Him that cometh to me I will in no wise cast out." That is as broad as the world itself. It takes that man in the gallery yonder; it may be there is a poor afflicted one hidden behind that post, it takes him; it just sweeps around this building, taking rich and poor alike—"Him that cometh to me I will in no wise cast out." He is so anxious to save sinners He will take every one who comes. He will take those who are so full of sin that they are despised by all who know them; who have been rejected by their fathers and mothers, who have been cast off by the wives of their bosoms. He will take those who have sunk so low that upon them no eye of pity is cast. "Him that cometh to me I will in no wise cast out." Now, why not take Him at His word? I remember a few years ago a man in Farwell Hall was greatly troubled about his soul. "Now," said I, "take that verse; what does the Lord mean when He says, 'Him that cometh to me I will in no wise cast out.' When He says that He means it." The man replied, "I will just take Him at His word." He started home, and while going over the Clark Street bridge, something whispered to him: "How do you know

but that is a wrong translation?" He was just laying right hold
of it when this was whispered to him. The poor fellow didn't
sleep any that night. He was greatly troubled, but at last he made
up his mind that he would just believe it, and when he got to the
Lamb of God he would tell Him of it, and the devil left him.
Now, my friends, just take it. Some men say, "I am not worthy
to come." I never knew a man yet to go to church that was
worthy. Why, He does not profess to save worthy men; He saves
sinners. As a man said in the inquiry-room: He didn't come to
save make-believe sinners—painted sinners, but real sinners. A
man don't want to draw his filthy rags of self-righteousness about
him when he comes to Him. The only thing a sinner has that
God wants is his sin. You need not bring your tears, your prayers,
your good works, or deeds; you must come to Him as a sinner,
and He will clothe you in a garment fit to come before Him. Now
the kings of this earth call around them the wealthy and influential men of their kingdom, but when Christ came down here He
called the outcasts, the publicans, and sinners around Him. And
that was the principal fault the people found with Him. Those
self-righteous Pharisees were not going to associate with harlots
and publicans. The principal charge against Him was: "This
man receiveth sinners and eateth with them." Who would have
such a man around him as John Bunyan in his time. He, a Bedford tinker, why he couldn't get inside one of the princely
castles. I was very much amused when I was over on the other
side. They had erected a monument to John Bunyan, and it was
unveiled by lords and dukes and great men. Why, while he was
on earth they wouldn't allow him inside the walls of their castles.
Yet he was made one of the mightiest instruments in the spread
of the gospel; no book that has ever been written comes so near
the Bible as John Bunyan's "Pilgrim's Progress." And he was a
poor Bedford tinker. So it is with God. He picks up some poor,
lost tramp, and makes him an instrument to turn hundreds and
thousands to Christ. It is a question whether in all Chicago there
is a man who is exercising such an influence for good as this man
Sawyer. Four years ago he was a tramp; he had been cast off by
his own mother, by his own sisters, by his wife, and he hadn't
seen his own son for fifteen years. Then he was a lost man. Cast

off by every one, but the Son of God stooped low enough to save him. I doubt, as I said before, whether there is a man who has so much influence as that man has to-day. "Him that cometh to me I will in no wise cast out." Is there some poor outcast some poor tramp, here to-night? I've got a good message for you. May be you are hiding away behind that post—I've got a good message for you, the best message you ever heard: "Him that cometh to me I will in no wise cast out." Come all—just as you are. Don't wait. He will take you as you sit into His loving bosom; He will make you a champion of the cross, and you will become an instrument in His hand to build up His kingdom. Thank God for such a book; thank God for such a gospel—thank the God of heaven for such a text: "Him that cometh to me I will in no wise cast out."

The next "I will" is found in Luke. We are told of a man who was full of leprosy; he was just rotten with it. Perhaps his fingers had rotted off; it might have been that his nose was eaten off. That is the way leprosy affects a man. Well, there is a man full of leprosy, and he comes to Christ just as he was. A good many people, if they had been in his place, would have waited till they got a little better before they came before Him; but this man wanted to get the leprosy away. If he had waited to see if he got better there would have been no sense in it. A man might as well, if he had a sick child, say, "When it gets better I will send for the doctor." It is because your child is sick that you want the doctor. It is because this man had the leprosy that he wanted Christ. The leper came to Him and said: "Lord, if thou wilt, thou canst make me clean." There is faith for you; and the Lord touched him, saying, "I will; be thou clean," and away went the leprosy as if it had been struck by lightning. I have often wondered if he ever turned around to see where it had gone; no doubt, like Naaman, his flesh became as the flesh of a little child. He didn't wait to see whether the leprosy would improve, because he was convinced it was growing worse and worse every day. So it is with you. You will never have a night so favorable for coming to Christ as this one. If you put off till tomorrow your sins will have become more numerous. If you wait till Sunday next a whole week's sins will be built upon those you have al-

ready. Therefore, the sooner you come the fewer sins you will
have to be forgiven. Come to Him to-night. If you say to Him,
"Lord, I am full of sin, Thou canst make me clean"; "Lord, I
have a terrible temper—Thou canst make me clean"; "Lord, I
have a deceitful heart—cleanse me, O God; give me a new heart,
O God; give me the power to overcome the flesh, and the snares
of the devil!" If you come to Him with a sincere spirit you will
hear the voice, "I will, be thou clean." It will be done. Do you
think that the God who created the world out of nothing, who
by a breath put life into the world—do you think that if He
says, "Thou wilt be clean," you will not? A great many people
say, "If I become converted, I am afraid I will not hold out."
Why, don't you see that we cannot serve God with our own
strength? When we accept Him He gives us strength to serve
Him. When He has taken away the leprosy of sin it is easy to
live for Him. And I want to call your attention to the fact that
even if you are bad He don't care. It may be that some one here
has disgraced his or her father or mother; it may be that they
have disgraced every friend they ever had, and that they just
despise themselves. Come to Him and He will cleanse you. It is
to you I am speaking to-night. He can save you to the uttermost.

The next "I will" I want to call your attention to is the "I
will" of confession in Matthew: "Whosoever therefore shall confess me before men, him will I confess also before my Father
which is in heaven." Let me say right here that this is the very
verse up to which men in Chicago have come. Men come to me
and say: "Do you mean to affirm, Mr. Moody, that I've got to
make a public confession when I accept Christ; do you mean to
say I've got to confess Him in my place of business; in my family;
am I to let the whole world know that I am on His side?" A
great many are willing to accept Christ, but they are not willing
to publish it, to confess it. A great many are looking at the lions
and the bears in the mountains. Now, my friends, the devil's
mountains are only made of smoke. Why, he can throw a straw
into your path and make a mountain of it. He says to you: "You
cannot confess and pray to your family; why, you'll break down.
You cannot tell it to your shopmate; he will laugh at you." But
when you accept Him you will have power to confess Him. He

has said: "If any man will come after me, let him deny himself, and take up his cross, and follow me." It is the way to heaven— by the way of the cross, and I believe in my soul that more men are stumbling upon this verse than upon any other. They are willing to do everything necessary except take up the cross and follow Him. Now, let me read this verse again: "Whosoever therefore shall confess me before men, him will I confess also before my Father which is in heaven." When I was in London there was a leading doctor in that city upwards of seventy years of age, wrote me a note to come and see him privately about his soul. He was living at a country seat a little way out of London, and he only came into town two or three times a week. He was wealthy and was nearly retired. I received the note right in the midst of the London work, and told him I could not see him. I received a note a day or two after from a member of his family urging me to come. The letter said his wife had been praying for him for fifty years, and all the children had become Christians by her prayers. She had prayed for him all those years, but no impression had been made upon him. Upon his desk they had found the letter from me, and they came up to London to see what it meant, and I said I would see him. When we met I asked him if he wanted to become a Christian, and he seemed every way willing, but when it came to confession to his family he halted. "I tell you," said he, "I cannot do that; my life has been such that I would not like to confess before my family." "Now there is the point; if you are not willing to confess Christ He will not confess you; you cannot be His disciple." We talked for some time, and he accepted. I found that while I had been in one room the daughter and some friends, anxious for the salvation of that aged parent, were in the other room praying to God, and when he started out, willing to go home and confess Christ, I opened the door of the other room, not knowing the daughter was there, and the first words she said were: "Is my father saved?" "Yes, I think he is," I answered, and ran down to the front door and called him back. "Your daughter is here," I said; "this is the time to commence your confession." The father, with tears trickling down his cheeks, embraced his child. "My dear daughter, I have accepted Christ," and a great flood of light broke upon him at that confession. A great many here in Chicago are ashamed to come out and take their stand for Christ. If you want peace and joy my friends, you must be willing to confess. I am told that in China the height of a Chinaman's ambition is to have his name put in the house of Confucius. He must have performed some great act of valor or done the State some great service before he can have his name there. That is the highest point of a Chinaman's ambition. It ought to be the height of our ambition to have our name registered in heaven and have Christ to confess us in the courts of heaven. How excited we used to be during the war when some general did something extraordinary, and some one got up in Congress to confess his exploits. How the papers used to talk about it. If we come out for Christ here He will confess us in heaven before the Throne and the angels. May God help you confess Him to-night.

Another "I will"—to me a very precious "I will"—was given to those early fishermen. He said: "If you will follow me I will make you fishers of men." That is the "I will" of service. I pity those Christians from the very depth of my heart, who have only made a profession of religion, and stopped there. My friends, they don't have the joy of salvation. I tell you the only happy Christians are those who are fishers of men. If a man be a true Christian he wins souls. He cannot help it, for He says, "If you will follow me I will make you fishers of men." Peter caught more men at Pentecost than he ever caught fish in his nets. I have often thought of the remark one of the disciples made to Him as they were standing together one day: "Lord, we have left all to follow thee." What did they leave? A few old fishing boats and broken nets. They were looking to those they had left behind, and a great many people here are looking to what they will leave if they serve Him. It is not necessary to leave the things of this life when you follow Him. It is not necessary to give up your business, if it's a legitimate one, in order to accept Christ. But you mustn't set your heart on the old nets by a good deal. Now, my friend, if you want to be a religious Christian, follow Him fully. No man follows Christ and ever regrets it, and the nearer we get to Him the more useful we become. Then we will save men. It seems to me after I am dead and gone I would rather have a man to come to my grave and drop a tear and say, "Here lies the man who converted me; who brought me to the cross of Christ"—it seems to me I would rather have this than a column of pure gold reaching to the skies built in my honor. If a man wants to be useful follow Him. You will succeed if you follow Him. Whenever you find a man who follows Christ you will find that man a successful one. He don't need to be a preacher, he don't need to be an evangelist to be useful. They may be useful in business. See what power an employer has if he likes. How he could labor with his employes and in his business relations. Often a man can be far more useful in a business sphere than he could in another. If we want to spend a life of usefulness, accept Him, and He will make you "fishers of men." Young man, don't you want to win souls to Christ? Well, then, just follow Him. "You follow me, and I will make you fishers of men."

The next "I will," a very precious one, is: "I will not leave you comfortless" down here in this dark world. Now some people think they have a very hard battle before them when they accept Him. A lady came to me lately and said, "I am the only one of my family, who is a Christian; and I feel lonely." "Why," said I, "Christ is with you; if you have got an elder sitting at the right hand of God what more do you want?" Oh, this precious "I will"; this comfort and joy, "I will be with you to the end of the world"; "I will never forsake you." You may take comfort to-night. He will be with you always. You may not see Him with the eye of flesh, but you will see Him by the eye of faith.

The next "I will" is found in the fourth chapter of John: "I will raise him up at the last day." These bodies of ours are going down to the grave, but they are not going to lie there long: the Son of God will wake it up. When He was here He raised up three bodies, and let me say to you, young children, that the first one He raised was a little child. Ah, there will be many little children there, "for of such is the kingdom of heaven." He gave us three instances. The first was the little girl. When the people heard He had raised up some one from the dead they thought it was a mistake. She wasn't dead; only asleep; it wasn't a real miracle. The next one was a young man. "Oh, no," they thought. "That's no miracle; if they had left him alone he'd have awoke;

he was only asleep." But the next case that came along was that of Lazarus, and Matthew tells us he had been dead four days—had been laid away in the sepulcher, and the Son of God merely said: "Lazarus, come forth." Now, I like a religion that gives me such comfort, that when I lay away any loved one in the grave, I know they will by and by hear the voice of the Son of God calling them forth. I used to wonder how Christians had so much comfort in affliction, and used to question whether I could have as much; but I have learned that God gives us comfort when we need it. A few weeks ago I stood at the grave of a man I loved more than any one on earth, except my wife and family. As he was laid down in the narrow bed and the earth dropped upon the coffin-lid, it seemed as if a voice came to me, saying: "He will rise again." I like a religion by which we can go to the grave of our loved ones and feel that they will rise again: I like a religion that tells us although we sow them in corruption they will rise incorruptible, that although we sow them in weakness they will rise in power and glory and ascend to the kingdom of light. This is the comfort for Christians. Thank God for this: "I will not leave you comfortless."

"I will that they may be with me" is the sweetest of all. The thought that I will see Him in His beauty; the thought that I will meet Him there, that I will spend eternity with Him, is the sweetest of them all. This last week we had Thanksgiving day. How many families gathered together, perhaps the first time in many years, and the thought would come stealing over some of them, who will be the first to break the circle? Perhaps many of these circles of friends will never meet again. Thank God yonder the circles shall never be broken—when the fathers and mothers and children gather around Him in those mansions into which death never enters, where sickness and sorrow never enter through yon pearly gates. Oh, thank God for this blessed religion—thank God for the blessed Christ; thank God for those blessed eight "I wills"—"Come unto me all ye that labour and are heavy laden, and I will give you rest"; "Him that cometh unto me I will in no wise cast out"; "Whosoever therefore shall confess me before men, him will I confess also before my father which is in heaven";

"If you will follow me I will make you fishers of men"; "I will, be thou clean"; "I will not leave you comfortless"; "I will that they may be with me." May God bless every soul in this building to-night, and bring you to the cross.

THE FRIEND OF THE SORROWING

LUKE 4:18

Preface

MR. MOODY, as anyone could easily believe who had any acquaintance with his published sermons, was greatly drawn to the text of this sermon, the wonderful words which our Lord pronounced concerning His own ministry quoted from Isaiah 61. There are nine illustrations in this sermon, in addition to five taken from the Scriptures, making a total of fourteen, probably more than he used in any other one sermon. The long illustration about this visit which Mr. Moody paid is not referred to in any biographical work known to me, which is only an illustration of what I have so often said and written that there are many, many interesting episodes in Mr. Moody's great career which, because they have never yet been used in any biography of Mr. Moody, await the careful attention of some future biographer who will give us a two or three-volume definitive life of the great evangelist. The same is true of Charles H. Spurgeon.

The sermon on this particular clause of the text is to be found in *Faith*, pp. 50-69 (two sermons); in *Glad Tidings* (1876) pp. 64-74; *London Discourses* (1875), pp. 138-48, and E. L. Pell, *Dwight L. Moody* (1900), pp. 356-74. Another part of the text was used for the sermon entitled "Deliverance of the Captives," which is in *Great Joy* (1879), pp .157-67; and *Sermons, Addresses, and Prayers* (1877), pp. 211-26 (two sermons). Another sermon from this text was "The Blind Whom Christ Would Heal" which is in *Gospel Awakening* (1879), pp. 165-79; and *Sermons, Addresses, and Prayers*, pp. 203-10, 227-36; another entitled "Restoring the Blind" is in *Sermons, Addresses, and Prayers*, pp. 231-36.

The Friend of the Sorrowing

LUKE 4:18: "He hath sent me to heal the broken-
hearted."

I WANT TO TAKE UP this one thought—that Christ was sent into
the world to heal the broken-hearted. When the Prince of Wales
came to this country a few years ago, the whole country was excited as to his purpose. What was his object in coming here?
Had he come to look into our republican form of government,
or our institutions, or was it simply to see and be seen? He came
and he went without telling us what he came for. When the
Prince of Peace came into this dark world He did not come in
any private way. He tells us that He came not to see and be
seen, but to "seek and to save that which was lost," and also "to
heal the brokenhearted." And in the face of this announcement
it is a mystery to me why those who have broken hearts will
rather carry them year in and year out than just bring them to
the great Physician. How many men in Chicago are just going
down to their graves with a broken heart? They have carried
their hearts weighted with trouble for years and years, and yet
when they open the Scriptures they can see the passage telling us
that He came here for the purpose of healing the brokenhearted.
He left Heaven and all its glory to come to the world—sent by
the Father, He tells us, for the purpose of healing the broken-
hearted.

You will find, my friends, that there is no class of people
exempt from broken hearts. The rich and the poor suffer alike.
There was a time when I used to visit the poor, that I thought
all the broken hearts were to be found among them; but within
the last few years I have found there are as many broken hearts
among the learned as the unlearned, the cultured as the un-
cultured, the rich as the poor. If you could but go up one of our
avenues and down another and reach the hearts of the people,
and get them to tell you their whole story, you would be aston-
ished at the wonderful history of every family. I remember a
few years ago I had been out of the city for some weeks. When
I returned I started out to make some calls. The first place I
went to I found a mother, her eyes red with weeping. I tried

to find out what was troubling her, and she reluctantly opened her heart and told me all. She said, "Last night my only boy came home about midnight drunk. I didn't know that he was addicted to drunkenness, but this morning I found out that he has been drinking for weeks, and," she continued, "I would rather have seen him laid in the grave than have had him brought home in the condition I saw him in last night." I tried to comfort her as best I could when she told me her sad story. When I went away from that house I didn't want to go into any other house where there was family trouble. The very next house I went to, however, where some of the children who attended my Sunday-school resided, I found that death had been there and laid his hand on one of them. The mother spoke to me of her affliction, and brought to me the playthings and the little shoes of the child, and the tears trickled down that mother's cheeks as she related to me her sorrow. I got out as soon as possible, and hoped I would see no more family trouble that day. The next visit I made was to a home where I found a wife with a bitter story. Her husband had been neglecting her for a long time, "and now," she said, "he has left me, and I don't know where he has gone. Winter is coming on, and I don't know what is going to become of my family." I tried to comfort her, and prayed with her, and endeavored to get her to lay all her sorrows on Christ. The next home I entered I found a woman crushed and broken-hearted. She told me her boy had forsaken her, and she had no idea where he had gone. That afternoon I made five calls, and in every home I found a broken heart. Every one had a sad tale to tell, and if you visited any home in Chicago you would find the truth of the saying that "there is a skeleton in every house." I suppose while I am talking you are thinking of the great sorrow in your own bosom. I do not know anything about you, but if I came round to every one of you, and you were to tell me the truth, I would hear a tale of sorrow. The very last man I spoke to last night was a young mercantile man, who told me his load of sorrow had been so great that many times during the last few weeks he had gone down to the lake and had been tempted to plunge in and end his existence. His burden seemed too much for him. Think of the broken hearts in Chicago to-night! They could be numbered by hundreds—yea, by thousands. All over this city are broken hearts. If all the sorrow represented in this great city was written in a book, this building couldn't hold that book, and you couldn't read it in a long lifetime. This earth is not a stranger to tears, neither is the present the only time when they could be found in abundance. From Adam's days to ours tears have been shed, and a wail has been going up to Heaven from the broken-hearted. And I say it again, it is a mystery to me how all those broken hearts can keep away from Him who has come to heal them. For six thousand years that cry of sorrow has been going up to God. We find the tears of Jacob put on record when he was told that his own son was no more. His sons and daughters tried to give him comfort, but he refused to be comforted. We are also told of the tears of King David. I can see him, as the messenger brings the news to him of the death of his son, exclaiming in anguish, "Oh, Absalom, my son, would that I had died for thee." And when Christ came into the world the first sound He heard was woe—the wail of those mothers in Bethlehem, and from the manger to the cross He was surrounded with sorrow. We are told that He often looked up to Heaven and sighed. I believe it was because there was so much suffering around Him. It was on His right hand and on His left—everywhere on earth; and the thought that He had come to relieve the people of the earth of their burdens, and so few would accept Him, made Him sorrowful. He came for that purpose. Let the hundreds of thousands just cast their burdens on Him. He has come to bear them as well as our sins. He will bear our griefs and carry our sorrow. There is not a burdened son of Adam in Chicago who can not but be freed if he will only come to Him. Let me call your attention to this little word "sent"—"He hath sent me." Take your Bibles and read about those who have been sent by God, and one thought will come to you—that no man who has ever been sent by God to do His work has ever failed. No matter how great the work, how mighty the undertaking; no matter how many difficulties had to be encountered, when they were sent from God they were sure to succeed. God sent Moses down to Egypt to bring three million people out of bondage. The idea would have seemed absurd to most people. Fancy a man with an impediment in his speech, without an army, without generals, with no record, bringing three million people from the power of a great nation like that of the Egyptians. But God sent him, and what was the result? Pharaoh said they should not go, and the great king and all his army were going to prevent them. But did he succeed? God sent Moses and he didn't fail. We find that God sent Joshua to the walls of Jericho, and he marched around the walls, and at the proper time these walls came tumbling down and the city fell into his hands. God sent Elijah to stand before Ahab, and we read the result. Samson and Gideon were sent by God, and we are told in the Scriptures what they accomplished; and so all through the Word we find that when God sent men they have never failed. Now, do you think for a moment that God's own Son, sent to us, is going to fail? If Moses, Elijah, Joshua, Gideon, Samson, and all those mighty men sent by God succeeded in doing their work, do you think the Son of Man is going to fail? Do you think, if He has come to heal broken hearts, He is going to fail? Do you think there is a heart so bruised and broken that can't be healed by Him? He can heal them all, but the great trouble is that men won't come. If there is a broken heart here to-night just bring it to the Great Physician. If you break an arm or a leg, you run off and get the best physician. If you have a broken heart you needn't go to a doctor or minister with it; the best physician is the Great Physician. In the days of Christ they didn't have hospitals or physicians as we have now. When a man was sick he was taken to the door, and the passersby prescribed for him. If a man came along who had had the same disease as the sufferer, he just told him what he had done to get cured. I remember I had a disease for a few months, and when I recovered if I met a man with the same disease I had to tell him what cured me; I could not keep the prescription all to myself. When He came there and found the sick at their cottage doors the sufferers found more medicine in His words than there was in all the prescriptions of that country. He is a mighty Physician who has come to heal every wounded heart in this building and in Chicago to-night. You needn't run to any other physician. The great difficulty is that people try to get some other physician—they go to this creed and that creed, to this doctor of divinity and that one, instead of coming directly to the Master. He has told us that His mission is to heal the broken hearts, and if He has said this, let us take Him at His word and just ask Him to heal.

I was thinking to-day of the difference between those who know Christ when trouble comes upon them and those who know Him not. I know several members of families in this city who are just stumbling into their graves over trouble. I know two widows in Chicago who are weeping and moaning over the death of their husbands, and their grief is just taking them to their graves. Instead of bringing their burdens to Christ, they mourn day and night, and the result will be that in a few weeks or years at most their sorrow will take them to their graves when they ought to take it all to the Great Physician. Three years ago a father took his wife and family on board that ill-fated French steamer. They were going to Europe, and when out on the ocean another vessel ran into her and she went down. That mother, when I was preaching in Chicago, used to bring her two children to the meetings every night. It was one of the most beautiful sights I ever looked upon to see how those little children used to sit and listen, and to see the tears trickling down their cheeks when the Saviour was preached. It seemed as if nobody else in that meeting drank in the truth as eagerly as those little ones. One night when an invitation had been extended to all to go into the inquiry-room, one of these little children said: "Mamma, why can't I go in too?" The mother allowed them to come into the room, and some friend spoke to them, and to all appearances they seemed to understand the plan of salvation as well as their elders. When that memorable night came, that mother went down and came up without her two children. Upon reading the news, I said: "It will kill her," and I quitted my post in Edinburgh—the only time I left my post on the other side—and went down to Liverpool to try and comfort her. But when I got there I found that the Son of God had been there before me, and instead of me comforting her, she comforted me. She told me she could not think of those children as being in the sea; it seemed as if Christ had permitted her to take those children on that vessel only that they might be wafted to Him, and had saved her life only that she might come back and work a little longer for Him. When she got up the other day at a mothers' meeting in Farwell Hall, and told her story, I thought I would tell the mothers of it the first chance I got. So if any of you have had some great affliction, if any of you have lost a loved and loving father, mother, brother, husband, or wife, come to Christ, because God has sent Him to heal the broken-hearted.

Some of you, I can imagine, will say, "Ah, I could stand that affliction; I have something harder than that." I remember a mother coming to me and saying, "It is easy enough for you to speak in that way; if you had the burden that I've got, you couldn't cast it on the Lord." "Why, is your burden so great that Christ can't carry it?" I asked. "No, it isn't too great for Him to carry, but I can't put it on Him." "That is your fault," I replied, and I find a great many people with burdens who, rather than just come to Him with them, strap them tighter on their backs and go away staggering under their load. I asked her the nature of her trouble, and she told me, "I have an only boy who is a wanderer on the face of the earth. I don't know where he is. If I only knew where he was I would go round the world to find him. You don't know how I love that boy. This sorrow is killing me." "Why can't you take him to Christ? You can reach Him at the throne, even though He be at the uttermost part of the world. Go tell God all about your trouble, and He will take away his sin, and not only that, but if you never see him on earth, God can give you faith that you will see your boy in Heaven." And then I told her of a mother who lived down in the southern part of Indiana. Some years ago her boy came up to this city. The boy was a moralist. My friends, a man has to have more than morality to lean upon in this great city. He hadn't been here long before he was led astray. A neighbor happened to come up here and found him one night in the streets drunk. When that neighbor went home, at first he thought he wouldn't say anything about it to the boy's father, but afterward he thought it was his duty to tell. So in a crowd in the street of their little town, he just took that father aside, and told him what he had seen in Chicago. It was a terrible blow. When the children had been put to bed that night he said to his wife, "Wife, I have bad news.

I have heard from Chicago to-day." The mother dropped her work in an instant, and said, "Tell me what it is." "Well, our son has been seen on the streets of Chicago drunk." Neither of them slept that night, but they took their burden to Christ, and about daylight the mother said: "I don't know how, I don't know when or where, but God has given me faith to believe that our son will be saved, and will never come to a drunkard's grave." One week after, that boy left Chicago. He couldn't tell why—an unseen power seemed to lead him to his mother's home, and the first thing he said on coming over the threshold was, "Mother, I have come home to ask you to pray for me"; and soon after, he came back to Chicago a bright and a shining light. If you have got a burden like this, fathers, mothers, bring it to Him and cast it on Him, and He, the Great Physician, will heal your broken hearts.

I can imagine, again, some of you saying, "How am I to do it?" My friends, go to Him as a personal friend. He is not a myth. What we want to do is to treat Christ as we treat an earthly friend. If you have sins, just go and tell Him all about them; if you have some great burden, "Go bury thy sorrow," bury it in His bosom. If you go to people and tell them of your cares, your sorrows, they will tell you they haven't time to listen. But He will not only hear your story, however long it be, but will bind up your broken heart. Oh, if there is a broken heart here to-night, bring it to Jesus, and I tell you upon authority He will heal you. He has said He will bind your wounds up—not only that, He will heal them.

During the war I remember of a young man not twenty, who was courtmartialed, down in the front, and sentenced to be shot. The story was this: The young fellow had enlisted. He was not obliged to, but he went off with another young man. They were what we would call "chums." One night this companion was ordered out on picket duty, and he asked the young man to go for him. The next night he was ordered out himself; and having been awake two nights, and not being used to it, fell asleep at his post, and for the offence he was tried and sentenced to death. It was right after the order issued by the President that no interference would be allowed in cases of this kind. This sort of thing had become too frequent, and it must be stopped. When the news reached the father and mother in Vermont it nearly broke their hearts. The thought that their son should be shot was too great for them. They had no hope that he would be saved by anything they could do. But they had a little daughter who had read the life of Abraham Lincoln, and knew how he loved his own children, and she said: "If Abraham Lincoln knew how my father and mother loved my brother he wouldn't let him be shot." That little girl thought this over, and made up her mind to see the President. She went to the White House, and the sentinel, when he saw her imploring looks, passed her in, and when she came up to the door and told the private secretary that she wanted to see the President, he could not refuse her. She came into the chamber and found Abraham Lincoln surrounded by his generals and counselors, and when he saw the little country girl he asked her what she wanted. The little maid told her plain, simple story— how her brother, whom her mother and father loved very dearly, had been sentenced to be shot. How they were mourning for him, and if he was to die in that way it would break their hearts. The President's heart was touched with compassion, and he immediately sent a dispatch canceling the sentence and giving the boy a parole so that he could come home and see that father and mother. I just tell you this to show you how Abraham Lincoln's heart was moved by compassion for the sorrow of that father and mother; and if he showed so much, do you think the Son of God will not have compassion upon you, sinner, if you only take that crushed, bruised heart to Him? He will heal it. Have you got a drunken husband? Go tell him. He can make him a blessing to the Church and to the world. Have you a profligate son? Go take your story to Him, and He will comfort you, and bind up and heal your sorrow. What a blessing it is to have such a Saviour. He has been sent to heal the broken-hearted. May the text, if the sermon doesn't, reach every one here to-night, and may every crushed, broken, and bruised heart be brought to that Saviour, and they will hear His comforting words. He will comfort you, as a mother comforts her child, if you will only come in prayer and lay all your burdens before Him.

THE NEW BIRTH

JOHN 3:3

Preface

IN ALL OF HIS CAMPAIGNS Mr. Moody was sure to emphasize over and over again the theme of regeneration, though he might preach on this from different texts. The text used here is from *Sermons, Addresses, and Prayers* (1877), pp. 121-26. Almost always Mr. Moody emphasizes in this sermon first of all what regeneration is not, giving five different experiences which must not be said to necessarily indicate regeneration, such as prayer, reading the Bible, etc. Though the sermon contains only four illustrations, I believe, 22 percent of the entire text is taken up with the last of these four illustrations, and this a hypothetical one. In some volumes where this sermon is printed, Mr. Moody gives an account of one of the unforgettable incidents of his chaplaincy during the Civil War.

This sermon is found in the following volumes: *Gospel Awakening* (1879), pp. 70-80; *Glad Tidings* (1876), pp. 86-97; *Holding the Fort*, pp. 81-97 (two sermons); *London Discourses* (1875), pp. 42-51; *Wondrous Love* (1875), pp. 27-40; and *To All People* (1877), pp. 416-26. For the most part, this is the sermon sometimes entitled "The Gateway into the Kingdom," which may be found in *The Way to God* (1884), pp. 23-41. It was separately published in 1875. See also *Bible Readings Delivered in San Francisco and Oakland* by D. L. Moody et al. (1881), pp. 186-91 (a very rare volume) .

On Being Born Again

JOHN 3:3: "Jesus answered and said unto him, Verily,
verily, I say unto thee, Except a man be born again,
he cannot see the kingdom of God."

SUPPOSE I PUT THE QUESTION to this audience, and ask how many
believe in the Word of God, I have no doubt every man and
every woman would rise and say, "I believe." There might be
an infidel or skeptic here and there, but undoubtedly the great
mass would say they believed. Then what are you going to do
with this solemn truth, "Except a man be born again, he cannot
see the kingdom of God," much less inherit it? There are a great
many mysteries in the Word of God. There are a great many
dark sayings of which we have not yet discovered the depth. But
God has put that issue so plainly and simply that he who runs
may read if he will. This third chapter of St. John makes the
way to Heaven plainer than any other chapter in the Bible; yet
there is no truth so much misunderstood, and the church and
the world are so troubled about, as this. Let me just say, before
I go any further, what regeneration is not. It is not going to
church. How many men think they are converted because they
go to church! I come in contact with many men who say they are
Christians because they go to church regularly. It is a wrong
idea that the devil never frequents any place but billiard-halls,
saloons, and theatres; wherever the Word of God is preached,
he is there. He is in this audience to-day. You may go to church
all the days of your life, and yet not be converted. Going to
church is not being born again. But there is another class who
say, "I don't place my hopes in going to church. I have been
baptized, and I think I was regenerated when that took place."
Where do those persons get their evidence? Certainly not in the
Bible. You cannot baptize men into regeneration. If you could, I
would go up and down the world and baptize every man, woman,
and child; and if I could not do it when they were awake, I would
do it while they slept. But the Word says, "Except a man be
born again"—born in the Spirit, born in righteousness from
above—"he cannot see the kingdom of God."

There is another class who say, "I was born again when I was confirmed. I was confirmed when I was five years old." But confirmation is not regeneration. A new birth must be the work of God, and not the work of man. Baptism, confirmation, and other ordinances are right in their place, but the moment you build hope on them instead of on new birth, you are being deceived by Satan. Another man says, "That is not what my hope is based upon; I say my prayers regularly." I suppose there was no man prayed more regularly than Paul did before Christ met him; he was a praying man. But saying prayers is one thing, and praying is another. Saying prayers is not conversion. You may pray from education; your mother may have taught you when you were a little boy. I remember that I could not go to sleep when I was a little boy unless I said my prayers, and yet perhaps the very next word I uttered might be an oath. There is just as much virtue in counting beads as in saying prayers, unless the heart has been regenerated and born again.

There is another class who say, "I read the Bible regularly." Well, reading the Bible is very good, and prayer is very good in its place; but you don't see anything in the Scriptures which says, "Except a man read the Bible he cannot see the kingdom of God." There is still another class who say, "I am trying to do the best I can, and I will come out all right." That is not new birth at all; that is not being born of God. Trying to do the best you can is not regeneration. This question of new birth is the most important that ever came before the world, and it ought to be settled in every man's mind. Every one should inquire, Have I been born of the Spirit? Have I passed from death unto life? Or am I building my hopes of Heaven on some form? In the first chapter of Genesis we find God working alone; He went on creating the world all alone. Then we find Christ coming to Calvary alone. His disciples forsook Him, and in redemption He was alone. And when we get to the third chapter of John we find that the work of regeneration is the work of God alone. The Ethiopian cannot change his skin, nor the leopard his spots; we are born in sin, and the change of heart must come from God. We believe in the good old Gospel.

What man wants is to come to God for this new heart. The moment he gets it he will work for the Lord. He cannot help it;

it becomes his second nature. Some say, "I would like to have you explain this new birth." Well, I might as well be honest, and own right up that I cannot explain it. I have read a great many books and sermons trying to explain the philosophy of it, but they all fail to do it. I don't understand how it is done. I cannot understand how God created the earth. It staggers me and bewilders me when I think how God created nature out of nothing. But, say the infidels, He did not do it. Then how did He do it? A man came to me in Scotland, and said he could explain it, and I asked him how those rocks are made. He said, "They are made from sand." "What makes the sand?" "Oh!" he replied, "Rocks." "Then," I asked him, "what made the first sand?" He couldn't tell. Not withstanding the philosophy of some people, we do believe that God did create the world. We believe in redemption. We believe that Christ came from the Father, and that He grew up and taught men. We believe He went into the sepulcher and burst the bands of death. You may ask me to explain all this; but I don't know how to do it. You ask me to explain regeneration. I cannot do it. But one thing I know—that I have been regenerated. All the infidels and skeptics could not make me believe differently. I feel a different man than I did twenty-one years ago last March, when God gave me a new heart. I have not sworn since that night, and I have no desire to swear. I delight to labor for God, and all the influences of the world cannot convince me that I am not a different man. I heard some time ago about four or five commercial travelers going to hear a minister preach. When they got back to their hotel, they began to discuss the sermon. A good many people just go to church for the purpose of discussing those things, but they should remember that they must be spiritually inclined to understand spiritual things. Those travelers came to the wise conclusion that the minister did not know what he was talking about. An old man heard them say they would not believe anything unless they could reason it out, and he went up to them and said: "While I was coming down in the train this morning I noticed in a field some sheep, some geese, some swine, and cattle eating grass. Can you tell me by what process that grass is turned into hair, feathers, wool, and horns?" "No," they answered, "not exactly." "Well, do you believe it is done?" "Oh, yes, we believe that." "But," said the old man, "you said you could not believe anything unless you understood it." "Oh," they answered, "we cannot help believing that; we see it." Well, I cannot help believing that I am regenerated, because I feel it. Christ could not explain it to Nicodemus, but said to him, "The wind bloweth where it listeth, and thou hearest the sound thereof, but canst not tell whence it cometh, and whither it goeth." Can you tell all about the currents of the air? He says it is every one that is born of the Spirit. Suppose, because I never saw the wind, I say it was all false. I have lived nearly forty years, and I never saw the wind. I never saw a man that ever did see it. I can imagine that little girl down there saying, "That man don't know as much as I do. Didn't the wind blow my hat off the other day? Haven't I felt the effects of the wind? Haven't I felt it beating against my face?" And I say you never saw the effects of the wind any more than a child of God felt the Spirit working in his heart. He knows that his eyes have been opened; that he has been born of the Spirit; that he has got another nature, a heart that goes up to God, after he has been born of the Spirit. It seems to me this is perfectly reasonable.

We have a law that no man shall be elected President unless he was born on American soil. I never heard any one complain of that law. We have Germans, Scandinavians, foreigners coming here from all parts of the world, and I never heard a man complain of that law. Haven't we got a right to say who shall reign? Had I any right when I was in England, where a Queen reigns, to interfere? Has a foreigner any right to interfere here? Has not the God of Heaven a right to say how a man shall come into His kingdom, and who shall come? And He says: "Except a man be born again, he cannot see the kingdom." How are you going to get in? Going to try to educate men? That is what men are trying to do, but it is not God's way. A man is not much better after he is educated if he hasn't got God in his heart. Other men say, "I will work my way up." That is not God's way, and the only way is God's way—to be born again. Heaven is a prepared place for a prepared people. You take an unregenerated man in Chicago and put him on the crystal pavements of Heaven, and it would be hell! A man that can't bear to spend one Sunday among God's people on earth, with all their imperfections, what is he going to do among those who have made their robes white in the blood of the Lamb? He would say that was hell for him. Take the unregenerated man and put him into the very shadow of the Tree of Life, and he wouldn't want to sit there. A man who is born of the Spirit becomes a citizen of another world. He has been translated into new life, taken out of the power of darkness, and translated into the Kingdom of Light. Haven't you seen all around you men who had become suddenly and entirely changed?

Just draw a picture: Suppose we go down into one of these alleys—and I have been into some pretty dark holes down here in this alley that used to lie back of Madison street, and I have seen some pretty wretched homes. Go to one of those rooms, and you find a wife, with her four or five children. The woman is heart-broken. She is discouraged. When she married that man he swore to protect, love, and care for her, and provide for all her wants. He made good promises and kept them, for a few years, and did love her. But he got led away into one of these drinking saloons. He was a noble-hearted man by nature, and those are just the ones that are led astray. He has now become a confirmed drunkard. His children can tell by his footfall that he comes home drunk. They look upon him as a monster. The wife has many a scar on her body that she has received from that man's arm who swore to love and protect her. Instead of being a kind-hearted husband, he has become a demon. He don't provide for that poor woman. What a struggle there is! And may God have mercy upon the poor drunkard and his family is my prayer constantly! Suppose he is here in that gallery up there, or in the dark back there, and you can't see him. May be he is so ashamed of himself that he has got behind a post. He hears that he may be regenerated; that God will take away the love of strong drink, and snap the fetters that have been binding him, and make him a free man, and he says, "By the grace of God I will ask Him to give me a new heart." And he says, "O God, save me!" Then he goes home. His wife says, "I never saw my husband look so happy for years. What has come over him?" He says, "I have been up there to hear these strangers. I heard Mr.

Sankey singing 'Jesus of Nazareth passeth by,' and it touched my heart. The sermon about being born again touched my heart, and, wife, I just prayed right there, and asked God to give me a new heart, and I believe He has done it. Come, wife, pray with me!" And there they kneel down and erect the family altar.

Three months hence you go to that home, and what do you find? All is changed. He is singing "Rock of Ages, cleft for me," or that other hymn his mother once taught him, "There is a fountain filled with blood." His children have their arms upon his neck. That is Heaven upon earth. The Lord God dwells there. That man is passed from death unto life. That is the conversion we are aiming at. The man is made better, and that is what God does when a man has the spirit of Heaven upon him. He regenerates them, re-creates them in His own image. Let us pray that every man here who has the love of strong drink may be converted. Unite in prayer with me now and ask God to save these men that are rushing on to death and ruin.

THERE IS NO DIFFERENCE

Romans 3:22

Preface

THIS SERMON was one Mr. Moody used with great frequency. It sometimes was entitled "Man's Great Failure." I would say that the word *failure* would be the characteristic theme of this message in which, probably more than in any other one sermon, he develops with great detail the doctrine of the total depravity of mankind. He crowds in a great many references from the Scriptures: he frequently refers to episodes in the book of Genesis, then takes material from Exodus, Numbers, and Joshua; he quotes from Jeremiah and the gospels, and other passages in the epistle to the Romans, and also, rather rare for Mr. Moody, he quotes from the book of Revelation. One is almost in the middle of the sermon before he comes upon any illustrations at all. This is the only place where I have found the illustration of the game by which arrows were shot through suspended rings. Here, as in so many of his sermons, he repeats the terrible experience through which he went in the great Chicago fire of 1871. In the text of a book published in 1889, Mr. Moody said, "I was led to take up this text tonight by what I heard last night in the inquiry-room. There was a moralist there—that is, he said he was a moralist—and he could not understand just how he was as bad as other people."

This above text is from Mr. Moody's *Select Sermons* (1881), pp. 22-40. It is also in *Gospel Awakening* (1879), pp. 179-84; *Great Redemption* (1889), pp. 171-84; *Glad Tidings* (1876), pp. 410-18; and *Moody's Great Sermons* (1899), pp. 234-47. This is the sermon that Mr. Barton inserted in the volume which he edited in 1901, *Pulpit Power and Eloquence,* pp. 517-21.

There Is No Difference

ROMANS 3:22

THAT IS ONE OF THE HARDEST TRUTHS man has to learn. We are apt to think that we are just a little better than our neighbors, and if we find *they* are a little better than ourselves, we go to work and try to pull them down to our level. If you want to find out who and what man is, go to the third chapter of Romans, and there the whole story is told. "There is none righteous, no, not one." "All have sinned, and come short." *All!* Some men like to have their lives written before they die. If you would like to read your biography, turn to this chapter, and you will find it already written.

I can imagine some one saying, "I wonder if he really pretends to say that 'there is no difference.'" The teetotaller asks, "Am I no better than the drunkard?' Well, I want to say right here that it is a good deal better to be temperate than intemperate; a good deal better to be honest than dishonest; it is better for a man even in this life to be upright in all his transactions than to cheat right and left. But when it comes to the great question of salvation, that does not touch the question at all, because "All have sinned, and come short of the glory of God." Men are all bad by nature; the old Adam stock is bad, and we cannot bring forth good fruit until we are grafted into the one True Vine. If I have an orchard, and two apple trees in it, which both bear some bitter apples, perfectly worthless, does it make any difference to me that the one tree has got perhaps five hundred apples, all bad, and the other only two, both bad? There is no difference. One tree has more fruit than the other, but it is all *bad*. So it is with man. One thinks he has got only one or two very little sins—God won't notice them; while another man has broken every one of the ten commandments! No matter, there is no difference; they are both guilty; they have both broken the law. The law demands complete and perfect fulfilment, and if you cannot do that, you are lost, as far as the law is concerned. "Whosoever shall keep the whole law, and yet offend in one point, he is guilty of all."

Suppose you were to hang up a man to the roof with a chain of ten links; if one were to break, does it matter that the other nine are all sound and whole? Not the least. One link breaks, and down comes the man. But is it not rather hard that he should fall when the other nine are perfect and only one is broken? Why, of course not; if one is broken, it is just the same to the man as if all had been broken; he falls. So the man who breaks one commandment is guilty of all. He is a criminal in God's sight. Look at yonder prison, with its thousand victims. Some are there for murder, some for stealing, some for forgery, some for one thing and some for another. You may classify them, but every man is a *criminal*. They have all broken the law, and they are all paying the penalty. So the law has brought every man in a criminal in the sight of God.

If a man should advertise that he could take a correct photograph of people's hearts, do you believe he would find a customer? There is not a man among us whom you could hire to have his photograph taken, if you could photograph the real man. We go to have our faces taken, and carefully arrange our toilet, and if the artist flatters us, we say, "Oh, yes, that's a first-rate likeness," as we pass it round among our friends. But let the real man be brought out, the photograph of the heart, and see if a man will pass that round among his neighbors. Why, you would not want your own wife to see it! You would be frightened even to look at it yourself.

Nobody knows what is in that heart but Christ. We are told that "the heart is deceitful above all things, and desperately wicked: who can know it?" We do not know our own hearts; none of us have any idea how bad they are. Some bitter things are written against me, but I know a good many more things about myself that are bad than any other man. There is nothing good in the old Adam nature. We have got a heart in rebellion against God by nature, and we do not even love God unless we are born of the Spirit. I can understand why men do not like this third chapter of Romans—it is too strong for them. It speaks the truth too plainly. But just because we do not like it, we shall be all the better for having a look at it; very likely we shall find that it is exactly what we want, after all. It's a truth that men do not at all like, but I have noticed that the medicine that we do not like is the medicine that will do us good. If we do not think we are as bad as the description, we must just take a closer look at ourselves.

Here is a man who thinks he is not just so bad as it makes him out to be. He is sure he is a little better than his neighbor next door; he goes to church regularly and his neighbor never goes to church at all! "Of course," he congratulates himself, "I'll certainly get saved easier." But there is no use trying to evade it. God has given us the law to measure ourselves by, and by this most perfect rule we have all sinned and come short, and "there is no difference."

Paul brings in the law to show man that he is lost and ruined. God, being a perfect God, had to give a perfect law, and the law was given not to save men, but to measure them by. I want you to understand this clearly, because I believe hundreds and thousands stumble at this point. They try to save themselves by trying to keep the law; but it was never meant for men to save themselves by. The law has never saved a single man since the world began. Men have been trying to keep it, but they have never succeeded, and never will. Ask Paul what it was given for. Here is his answer, "That every mouth might be stopped, and the whole world become guilty before God." In this third chapter of Romans the world has been put on trial, and found guilty. The verdict has been brought in against us all—ministers and elders and church members, just as much as prodigals and drunkards—"ALL have sinned and come short."

The law stops every man's mouth. God will have a man humble himself down on his face before Him, with not a word to say for himself. Then God will speak to him, when he owns that he is a sinner, and gets rid of his own righteousness. I can always tell a man who has got near the kingdom of God; his mouth is stopped. If you will allow me the expression, God always shuts up a man's lips before He saves him. Job was not saved until he stopped talking about himself. Just see how God deals with him. First of all, He afflicts him, and Job begins to talk about his own goodness. "I delivered the poor," he says, "and the fatherless, and him that had none to help him. I was eyes to the

blind, and feet was I to the lame. I was a father to the poor!"
Why, they would have made Job an elder, if there had been
elders in those days! He was a wonderfully good man! But
now God says, "I'll put a few. questions to you. Gird up now
thy loins like a man; for I will demand of thee, and answer thou
me." And Job is down directly; he is ashamed of himself; he
cannot speak of his works any more. "Behold," he cries, "I am
vile; what shall I answer thee? I will lay mine hand upon my
mouth." But he is not low enough yet, perhaps, and God puts a
few more questions. "Ah," says Job, "I never understood these
things before—I never saw it in that light." He is thoroughly
humbled now; he can't help confessing it. "I have heard of thee
by the hearing of the ear: but now mine eye seeth thee. *Wherefore I abhor myself, and repent in dust and ashes.*" Now he has
found his right position before God, and now God can talk to
him. And God helps him, and raises him up, and gives him the
double of all that he had before. The clouds and the mist and
the darkness around his path are driven away, and light from
eternity bursts into his soul when he sees his nothingness in the
sight of a pure and holy God.

This, then, is what God gives us the law for—to show us ourselves in our true colors.

I said to my family one morning a few weeks before the Chicago fire, "I am coming home this afternoon to give you a ride."
My little boy clapped his hands. "Oh, papa, will you take me to
see the bears in Lincoln Park?" "Yes." You know boys are very
fond of seeing bears. I had not been gone long when my little
boy said, "Mamma, I wish you would get me ready." "Oh," she
said, "it will be a long time before papa comes." "But I want to
get ready, mamma." At last he was ready to have the ride, face
washed, and clothes all nice and clean. "Now, you must take
good care and not get yourself dirty again," said mamma. Oh, of
course he was going to take care; he wasn't going to get dirty.
So off he ran to watch for me. However, it was a long time yet
until the afternoon, and after a little he began to play. When I
got home, I found him outside, with his face all covered with
dirt. "I can't take you to the Park that way, Willie." "Why,
papa? You said you would take me." "Ah, but I can't; you're

covered with mud. I couldn't be seen with such a dirty little boy." "Why I'se clean, papa; mamma washed me." "Well, you've got dirty since." But he began to cry, and I could not convince him that he was dirty. "I'se clean; mamma washed me!" he cried. Do you think I argued with him? No. I just took him up in my arms, and carried him into the house, and showed him his face in the looking-glass. He had not a word to say. He would not take my word for it, but one look at the glass was enough; he saw it for himself. He didn't say he wasn't dirty after that!

Now the looking-glass showed him that his face was dirty—*but I did not take the looking-glass to wash it;* of course not. Yet that is just what thousands of people do.

THE LAW IS THE LOOKING-GLASS

to see ourselves in to show us how vile and worthless we are in the sight of God; but people take the law, and try to *wash* themselves with it! Man has been trying that for six thousand years, and has miserably failed. *By the deeds of the law there shall no flesh be justified in His sight.* Only one Man ever lived on the earth who could say He had kept the law, and that was the Lord Jesus Christ. If he had committed one sin, and come short in the smallest degree, His offering Himself for us would have been useless. But men have tried to do what He did, and have failed. Instead of sheltering under His righteousness, they have offered God their own. And God knew what a miserable failure it would be. "There is none righteous, no not one."

I don't care where you put man, everywhere he has been tried he has proved a total failure. He was put in Eden on trial. Some men say they wish they had Adam's chance. If they had, they would go down as quickly as he did. Put five hundred children into a hall, and give them ten thousand toys. Tell them they can run all over the hall, and they can have anything they want except one thing, placed, let us say, in one of the corners of Mr. Sankey's organ. Go out for a little, and do you not think that is the very first place they will go to? Why, nothing else in the room would have any attraction for them but just the thing they were told not to touch. And so let us not think Adam was any worse than ourselves. Adam was put on trial, and Satan walked into Eden. I do not know how long he was there, but I should think he had not been there twenty minutes before he stripped Adam of everything he had. There he is, fresh from the hands of his Creator; Satan comes upon the scene, and presents a temptation, and down he goes. *He was a failure.*

Then God took man into covenant with Him. He said to Abraham, "Look yonder at the stars in the heavens and the sands on the seashore; I will make your seed like those. I will bless thee and multiply thee upon the earth." But what a stupendous failure man was under the covenant! Go back and read about it.

The Israelites are brought out of Egypt, see many signs and wonders, and stand at last at the foot of Mount Sinai. Then God's holy law is given to them. Did they not promise to keep it? "O yes," they cry, "we'll keep the law." To hear them talk you might think it was going to be all right now. But just wait till Joshua and Moses have turned their backs! No sooner have their leaders gone up the mountain to have an interview with God than they begin to say, "We wonder what has become of this man, Moses? We don't know where he has gone to. Come, let us make unto us another god. Aaron, make us a golden calf! Here are the golden ornaments we got from the Egyptians. Come and make us another god!" When it is made, the people raise a great shout, and fall down and worship it. "Hark! Listen; what shout is that I hear?" says Moses, as he comes down the mountain side. "Alas," says Joshua, "there's war in the camp; it is the shout of the victor." "Ah no," says Moses, "it isn't the shout of victory or of war, Joshua; it is the cry of idolaters. They have forgotten the God who delivered them from the Egyptians, who led them through the Red Sea, who fed them with bread from heaven—angels' food. They have forgotten their promises to keep the commandments. Already the first two of them are broken, 'no other gods,' 'no graven image.' They've made them another god—a golden god!" And that's what men have been doing ever since.

Men worship the golden calf rather than the God of heaven. Look around you. They bring before it health, and happiness, and peace. "Give me thirty pieces of silver, and I will sell you Christ," is the world's cry today. "Give me fashion, and I will

sell you Christ!" "I will sacrifice my wife, my children, my life,
my all, for a little drink. I will sell my soul for drink!" It is
easy to blame those Israelites for worshiping the golden calf.
But what are we doing ourselves? Ah, man was a *failure* then,
and he has been a failure ever since.

Then God put him under the judges, and wonderful judges
they were; but, once more, what a failure he was! After that came
the prophets, and what a failure he was under them! Then came
the Son Himself from heaven out of the bosom of the Father.
He left the throne and came down here to teach us how to live.
We took Him and murdered Him on Calvary! Man was a *failure*
in Christ's time.

And now we are living under the dispensation of grace—a
wonderful dispensation. God is showering down blessings from
above. But what is man under grace? A stupendous failure.
Look at that man reeling on his way to a drunkard's grave, and
his soul going to a drunkard's hell! Look at the wretched harlots
on your streets! Look at the profligacy and the pauperism and
the loathsome sickness! Look at the vice and crime that fester
everywhere, and tell me is it not true that man is a *failure* under
grace?

Yes, man is a failure. I can see down the other side of the
millennium. Christ has swayed His sceptor over the earth for a
thousand years; but man is a failure still for "when the thousand years are expired, Satan shall be loosed out of his prison,
and shall go out to deceive the nations which are in the four
quarters of the earth, Gog and Magog, to gather them together
to battle . . . and they . . . compassed the camp of the saints
about, and the beloved city: and fire came down from God out
of heaven, and devoured them." What man, wants is another
nature; he must be born again. What a foolish saying. "Experience teaches." Man has been a long time at that school, and has
never learned his lesson yet—his own weakness and inability.
He still thinks great things of his own strength. "I am going
to stand after this," he says, "I have hit upon the right plan this
time. I am able to keep the law now." But the first temptation
comes, and he is down. Man will not believe in God's strength.

Man will not acknowledge himself a failure, and surrender to Christ to save him from his sins.

Is it not better to find out in this world that we are a failure, and to go to Christ for deliverance, than to sleep on and go down to hell without knowing we are sinners?

I know this doctrine that we have all failed, that we have all sinned and come short, is exceedingly objectionable to the natural man. If I had tried to find out the most disagreeable verse in the whole Bible, perhaps I could not have fastened upon one more universally disliked than *"There is no difference."*

I can imagine Noah leaving his ark and going off preaching once in a while. As the passers-by stop to listen, there is no sound of the hammer or the plane. Noah has stopped work. He has gone off on a preaching tour, to warn his countrymen. Perhaps he tells them that a great deluge is coming to sweep away all the workers of iniquity; perhaps he warns them that *every* man who is not in the ark must perish; that there would be *no difference.* I can imagine one man saying, "You had better go back and finish your work, Noah, rather than come here preaching. You don't think we are going to believe in such nonsense as that! You tell us that all are going to perish alike! Do you really expect us to believe that the kings and governors, the sheriffs and the princes, the rulers, the beggars and thieves and harlots, are all going to be alike lost?" "Yes," says Noah; "the deluge that is coming by and by will take you all away—every man that is not in the ark must die. There will be no difference." Doubtless they thought Noah had gone raving mad. But did not the flood come and take them all away? Princes and paupers, and knaves and kings—was there any difference? No difference.

When the destroying angel was about to pass through Egypt, no doubt the haughty Egyptian laughed at the poor Israelite putting the blood on his door-post and lintel. "What a foolish notion," he would say, derisively; "the very idea of sprinkling blood on a door-post! If there *were* anything coming, that would never keep it away. I don't believe there is any death coming at all; and if it did, it might touch these poor people, but it would certainly never come near us." But when the night came, there was no difference. The king in his palace, the captive in his prison, the beggar by the wayside—they were all alike. Into every house the king of terrors had come, and there was universal mourning in the land. In the home of the poor and the lowly, in the home of the prince and the noble, in the home of governor and ruler, the eldest son lay dead. Only the poor Israelite escaped who had the blood on the door-post and lintel. And when God comes to us in judgment, if we are not in Christ, all will be alike. Learned or unlearned, high or low, priest or scribe —there will be no difference.

Once more, I can imagine Abraham going down from the hills to Sodom. He stands up, let us say, at the corners of the streets, before Sodom was destroyed—"Ye men of Sodom, I have a message from my God to you." The people stand and look at the old man—you can see his white locks as the wind sweeps through them. "I have a warning for you," he cries; "God is going to destroy the five cities of the plain, and every man who does not escape to yonder mountain must perish. When He cames to deal in judgment with you there will be no difference; every man must die. The Lord Mayor, the princes, the chief men, the mighty men, the judges, the treasurers—all must perish. The thief and the vagabond, and the drunkard—yes, all must perish alike. There can be 'no difference.'" But these Sodomites answer, "You had better go back to your tent on the hills, Abraham. We don't believe a word of it. Sodom was never so prosperous. Business was never so flourishing as now. The sun never shone any brighter than it does today. The lambs are skipping on the hills, and everything moving on as it has done for centuries. Don't preach that stuff to us; we don't believe it." A few hours pass, and Sodom is in ashes! Did God make any difference among those who would not believe? No, God never utters any opinion; what He says is truth. "All have sinned and come short," He cries; "and there is no difference." I read of a deluge of fire that is going to roll over this earth, and when God comes to deal in judgment, there will be no difference, and every man who is out of Christ must perish.

It was my sad lot to be in the Chicago fire. As the flames rolled down our streets, destroying everything in their onward march, I saw the great and the honorable, the learned and the wise, fleeing before the fire with the beggar and the thief and the harlot. All were alike. As the flames swept through the city it was like the judgment day. Neither the mayor, nor the mighty men, nor the wise man could stop those flames. They were all on a level then, and many who were worth hundreds of thousands were left paupers that night. When the day of judgment comes, there will be no difference. When the deluge came there was no difference; Noah's ark was worth more than all the world. The day before, it was the world's laughing-stock and if it had been put up to the auction, you could not have got anybody to buy it except for firewood. But the deluge came, and then it was worth more than all the world together. And when the day of judgment comes, Christ will be worth more than all this world, more than ten thousand worlds. And if it was a terrible thing in the days of Noah to die outside the ark, it will be far more terrible for us to go down in our sins to a Christless grave.

Now I hope that you have seen what I have been trying to prove—that

We Are All Sinners Alike

I should like to use another illustration or two. I should like to make this truth so plain that a child might know it.

In the olden times in England, we are told, they used to have a game of firing arrows through a ring on the top of a pole. The man that failed to get all his arrows through the ring was called a "sinner." Now I should like for a moment to take up that illustration. Suppose our pole to be up in the gallery, and on the top of it the ring. I have got ten arrows, let us say, and Mr. Sankey has got another ten. I take up the first arrow, and take a good aim. Alas! I miss the mark. Therefore I am a "sinner." "But," I say, "I will do the best I can with the other nine. I have only missed with one." Like some men who try to keep all the commandments but one! I fire again, and miss the mark a second time. "Ah, but," I say, "I have got eight arrows still," and away goes another arrow—miss! I fire all the ten arrows and do not get one through the ring. Well, I was a "sinner" after the first miss, and I can only be a "sinner" after the tenth. Now Mr. Sankey comes with his ten arrows. He fires and gets his first arrow through. "Do you see that?" he says. "Well," I reply, "go on; don't boast until you get them all through." He takes the second arrow and gets that through. "Ha! Do you see that?" "Don't boast," I repeat, "until all ten are through." If a man has not broken the law at all he has got something to boast of! Away goes the third, and it goes through. Then another and another all right, and another until nine are through. "Now," he says, "one more arrow, and I am not a sinner." He takes up the last arrow, his hand trembles a little; he *just misses* the mark. *And he is a "sinner" as well as I am.*

My friend have you never missed the mark? Have you not come short? I should like to see the man who never missed the mark. *He never lived.*

Let me give you just one more illustration. When Chicago was a small town, it was incorporated and made a city. When we got our charter for the city, there was one clause in the constitution that allowed the Mayor to appoint all the police. It worked very well when it was a small city; but when it had three or four hundred thousand inhabitants, it put too much power in the hands of one man. So our leading citizens got a new bill passed that took the power out of the hands of the Mayor, and put it into the hands of Commissioners appointed by government. There was some clause in the new law that no man should be a policeman who was not a certain height—5 feet 6 inches, let us say. When the Commissioners got into power, they advertised for men as candidates, and in the advertisement they stated that no man need apply who could not bring good credentials to recommend him. I remember going past the office one day, and there was a crowd of men waiting to get in. They quite blocked up the side of the street, and they were comparing notes as to their chances of success. One said to another, "I have got a good letter from Senator So-and-so. I'm sure to get in." The two men come on together, and lay their letters down on the Commissioner's desk. "Well," say the officials, "you have certainly a good many letters, but we won't read them till we measure you." Ah! They forgot all about that. So the first man is measured, and he is only five feet. "No chance for you, sir. The law says the man must be 5 feet 6 inches, and you don't come up to the standard." The other says, "Well, my chance is a good deal better than his, I'm a good bit taller than he is"—and he begins to measure himself by the other man. That is what people are always doing, measuring themselves by others. Measure yourselves by the law of God, or by the Son of God Himself; and if you do that, you will find you have come short. He goes up to the officers, and they measure him; 5 feet 5 inches and nine-tenths of an inch. "No good," they tell him; "you're not up to the standard." "But I'm only one-tenth of an inch short," he remonstrates. "It's no matter," they say; "there's no difference." He goes with the man who was five feet. One comes short six inches, and the other only one-tenth of an inch, but the law cannot be changed. And the law of God is that no man shall go into the kingdom of heaven with *one* sin on him. He that has broken the least law is guilty of all.

"Then, is there any hope for me?" you say. "What star is there to relieve the midnight darkness and gloom? What is to become of me? If all this is true, I am a poor lost soul. I have committed sin from my earliest childhood."

Thank God, my friends, this is just where the gospel comes in. "He was made sin for us, who knew no sin." "He was wounded for our transgressions, he was bruised for our iniquities: the chastisement of our peace was upon him; and with his stripes we are healed." "All we like sheep have gone astray; we have turned every one to his own way, and the Lord *hath laid* on him the iniquity of us all."

You ask me what my hope is; it is that Christ died for my sins, in my stead, in my place, and therefore I can enter into life eternal. You ask Paul what his hope was. "Christ died for our sins according to the scriptures." This is the hope in which died all the glorious martyrs of old, in which all who have entered heaven's gate have found their only comfort. Take that doctrine of substitution out of the Bible, and my hope is lost. With the law, without Christ, we are all undone. The law we have broken, and it can only hang over our head the sharp sword of justice. Even if we could keep it from this moment, there remains the unforgiven past. "Without shedding of blood is no remission."

There is a well-known story told of Napoleon the First's time. In one of the conscriptions, during one of his many wars, a man was balloted as a conscript who did not want to go, but he had a friend who offered to go in his place. His friend joined the regiment in his name, and was sent off to the war. By and by a battle came on, in which he was killed, and they buried him on the battlefield. Some time after, the emperor wanted more men, and by some mistake the first man was balloted a second time. They went to take him, but he remonstrated. "You cannot take me." "Why not?" "I am dead," was the reply. "You are not dead; you are alive and well." "But I *am* dead," he said. "Why, man, you must be mad! Where did you die?" "At such a battle, and you left me buried on such a battlefield." "You talk like a madman," they cried; but the man stuck to his point that he had been dead and buried some months. "Look up your books," he said, "and see if it is not so." They looked, and found that he was right. They found the man's name entered as drafted, sent to the war, and marked off as killed. "Look here," they said, "you didn't die. You must have got some one to go for you. It must have been your *substitute.*" "I know that," he said; "he died in my stead. You cannot touch me. I died in that man, and now I go free. The law has no claim against me." They would not recognize the doctrine of substitution, and the case was carried to the emperor, who said that the man was right, that he was dead and buried in the eyes of the law, and that France had no claim against him.

The story may be true, or may not, but one thing I know to be true, that the Emperor of heaven recognizes the doctrine of substitution. Christ died for me; that is my hope of eternal life. "There is no condemnation to them which are in Christ Jesus." If you ask me what you must do to share this blessing, I answer— go and deal personally with Christ about it. Take the sinner's place at the foot of the cross. Strip yourself, of all your own righteousness, and put on Christ's. Wrap yourself up in His perfect robe, and receive Him by simple trust as your own Saviour. Thus you inherit the priceless treasures that Christ hath purchased with His blood. *"As many as received him, to them gave he power to become the sons of God."* Yes, sons of God: power to overcome the world, the flesh, and the devil; power to crucify every besetting sin, passion, lust; power to shout in triumph over every trouble and temptation of your life, "I can do all things through Christ which strengtheneth me."

I have been trying to tell you the old, old tale that men are sinners. I may be speaking to some one, perhaps, who thinks it a waste of time. "God knows I'm a sinner," he cries; "you don't need to prove it. Since I could speak, I've done nothing but break every law of earth and heaven." Well, my friend, I have good news for you. It is just as easy for God to save you who have broken the whole decalogue, as the man who has only broken one of the commandments. Both are dead—dead in sins. It is no matter how *dead* you are, or how long you have been dead; Christ can bring you to life just the same. There is no difference. When Christ met that poor widow coming out of Nain, following the body of her darling boy to the grave—he was just newly dead—His loving heart could not pass her; He stopped the funeral, and bade the dead arise. He was obeyed at once, and the mother was clasped once more in the living embrace of her son. And when Jesus stood by the grave of Lazarus, who had been dead *four* days, was it not just as easy for Him to say, "Lazarus, come forth"? Was it not as easy for Him to bring Lazarus from his tomb, who had been dead four days, as the son of the widow, who had been dead but one? Yes, it was just as easy; there was no difference. They were both alike dead, and Christ raised the one just as easily, and as willingly, and as lovingly as the other. And therefore, my friend, you need not complain that Christ cannot save you. Christ died *for the ungodly,* and if you turn to Him at this moment with an honest heart, and receive Him simply as your Saviour and your God I have the authority of His Word for telling you that He will *in no wise. cast you out.*

And you who have never felt the burden of your sin—you who think there is a great deal of difference—you who thank God that you are not as other men—beware! God has nothing to say to the self-righteous. Unless you humble yourself before Him in the dust, and confess before Him your iniquities and sins, the gate of heaven, which is open only for *sinners saved by grace,* must be shut against you forever!

"WHAT SEEK YE?"

John 1:38

Preface

CONFINING OURSELVES to the sermons of Mr. Moody that have appeared in print, one discovers that he preached more often from the gospels of Luke and John, using twenty different texts from each of these gospels, than from any other portion of the Word of God. There are only six illustrations in this sermon, yet they embrace more than one-third of the entire text. Although this sermon is not one of his greatest, it is one which he very frequently preached.

I do not know the date it occurred, but Mr. Moody begins a long illustration with the words, "When the Lawrence Mills were on fire, a number of years ago." We have also a good example here of how he often considerably altered later sermons on a given text. Thus, for example, in his sermon on these two texts appearing in the volume entitled *The Great Redemption*, which records all of his sermons and addresses, delivered in the Cleveland Tabernacle during the fall of 1879, all of these illustrations are omitted except the one regarding his friend who would not give his heart to Christ when he heard sermons on Matthew 6:33. Only in the later sermon, two and a half pages are used to record this very moving incident. The earlier account of this sermon practically closes with this illustration, but in the later report it appears in the middle of the sermon, and Mr. Moody closed with a strong appeal ending, "If there was only one thing to ask for you would ask for eternal life. It is a great thing to live forever. There is not anything to be compared with eternal life. . . ."

The text used here is from *Moody's Great Sermons* (1899), pp. 107-17. It also appeared in *Gospel Awakening* (1879), pp. 299-305; *Glad Tidings* (1876), pp. 263-72; and *Sermons, Addresses, and Prayers* (1877), pp. 245-54.

"What Seek Ye?"

I HAVE FOR MY SUBJECT this afternoon a question, a command
and an invitation. In the first chapter of John and the 38th verse,
it is related that Christ turned to two of John the Baptist's disciples, about four o'clock in the afternoon, who were following
Him, and said to them: "What seek ye?" The first words that
fell from the lips of the Son of God, as He commenced His ministry—that is John's account of it—were: "What seek ye?"

There were all classes of people following Christ while He
was upon earth. There were some that went to see Him just out
of a morbid curiosity—they had no other motive. There were
some who went for the fishes and the loaves. There was another
class that followed Him that they might get mere temporal relief;
that they might get some friend healed. Then there was another
class that followed Him that they might entangle Him in some
conversation; they were constantly putting difficult questions to
Him in hopes that they might get Him to say something against
the law of Moses that they might condemn Him and put Him to
death. There were some that went just to see, and others that
went to be seen. Here and there were some that followed Him
for just what He was to them, and they always got a blessing.

Now I contend that all the men and women in Cleveland are
seeking something. The question that I want to press home upon
you to-day is, "What seek ye?" What brought you out here this
afternoon? I venture to say if this audience could be sifted to
find out who had come to get a blessing, it would be found to be
a very small number; there would be vacant chairs enough;
there would be no trouble about room for the people that wanted
to come.

Although eighteen hundred years have rolled away since Christ
put that question to those disciples, human nature has not
changed. You will find the same classes now. There are some
that have come just out of curiosity—just merely to see and to be
seen. Some have come because they have been persuaded by a
godly mother to come. They did not come because they wanted
to, but because a mother, or a wife, or a little child had persuaded them, and they have come just to please them.

One man in Philadelphia got up at the young converts' meeting and said he did not come to hear the preaching or the singing. He said that a friend of his got there one night at the opening of the depot building, and he said he thought it was a remarkable scene to see eleven thousand chairs all vacant. He said he would like to see eleven thousand chairs in one building. So he went up late in the afternoon or early in the evening. He was the first one there, and the moment the doors were open he rushed in to see the empty chairs. That was what brought him there. Pretty high motive, wasn't it? He was a drinking man. The text that night was, "Where art thou?" and he saw something else before the meeting was over. He saw himself a poor, blind, miserable, wretched sinner. I hope some one that has come here to-day out of curiosity will get his eyes opened, and if you do you may get something you did not come for—something worth more than all this world to you.

When we were in London a man was going by Agricultural Hall, and it was raining pretty hard, and he dropped in just to get out of the rain, and the word reached him where he stood, and he was convicted and converted.

It is astonishing what motives bring a class of people together. You know and God knows what brought you here. What is the motive? Have you come merely to gratify curiosity? Have you come to gratify some friends? "What seek ye?"

I can imagine some of you say, "I did not come here to hear you preach. I came to hear the singing. I am very fond of music, and I would like to hear the singing, and I just wish that I was out of here; I don't like sermons; I just hate them." Well, I am glad you came for that motive, and I am thankful there is gospel enough in some of these hymns to save you. So if you did not come for any higher motive than to see or be seen, or hear the singing, we are glad to see you. But if you just change the motive and say, "I want a blessing. I want God to bless me. I want Him above everything else," this will be the happiest day you ever spent on earth.

Now, let us take the question home. What brought us here? "What seek ye?" Have you come to get Jesus Christ? If you have you can find Him. You have not got to go up to bring Him down. You have not got to go down to bring Him up. He is right here.

I want to tell you another thing: It is a command for you to seek Him, and I want to lay that command right across every man's path here to-day. "Seek first the kingdom of God and his righteousness, and all things else shall be added." What man puts first, God puts last; or reversed, what God puts first, man puts last.

If I should ask a good many of you to-day why you do not seek the kingdom of God, you would make me this answer, "Well, I have a good many other things to attend to. My business has got to be looked after; times are hard; times have been hard for the last five years; and don't you know, Mr. Moody, a man is worse than an infidel if he don't provide for his family?" So he is; no doubt about that, but then here is a command. God never makes any mistakes. He does not command us to do something that He does not give us power to do. If He commands all men now everywhere to repent, He means it. If He commands me to seek first the kingdom of God, I am to seek it first; I am to do that above everything else.

I am one of those that firmly believe that a man is just as good a business man in whom the kingdom of God is set up, as a man that goes on serving the world, living for the world. I believe a man is not fit to live—is not qualified for business—until he has obeyed God. I believe God turns the ways of the wicked upside down, and hedges up their way. Some one will say, "I have seen some of the wickedest men in this country get very rich." So have I. But then a man may get very rich and not be very prosperous after all. All is not gold that glitters. A man may have great wealth and not have contentment. A man may have great wealth and not have peace of mind. A man may have great wealth and be a stranger to rest. If I wanted to find a skeleton, I would go up here on your fine avenues, into some of those palaces there. You have not got to go down into your brothels and dark dens of iniquity, and your wretched homes, made dark by sin. You will find them there, I admit; but you will find them also in the homes of the fashionable, and in the palaces of the wealthy. There is hardly a family in the city that has not a skeleton in it. I believe that the reason that there is so much darkness and misery in this world is because men and women go contrary to what God tells them. About the last thing a man thinks of seeking is the kingdom of God. If you talk with a great many they will say they must attend to their business. They will tell you that when they get settled in life and have time, then they will attend to their soul's interests.

Now, when we start out in life, it is better that we start right. When God tells me to run, I am to run. When He tells me to walk, I am to walk. If He tells me to believe, I am to believe. If He tells me to seek first the kingdom of God, I must do it. No man or woman is justified in going out of this hall to-day without seeking the kingdom of God. If you go out of this hall without doing it, you trample one of God's commands under your feet. Some people think they never break a commandment. We have something besides the decalogue. This commandment is just as binding as the commandment, "Thou shalt not steal." It is a command from God, "Seek ye first the kingdom of God." Man says, "I will not do it. I will seek for pleasure. I will seek for wealth. I will seek for honor. I will seek for fame. I will seek for everything else before I will seek the kingdom of God." Is not that true? Don't we see that all around us? They are just living in disobedience. You know if you have a child that disobeys you, you will not want that child to prosper. You do not want your child to prosper in disobedience. But when a child is obedient, then you love to see the child prosper. Now, as long as we live in disobedience to God, how can we expect to prosper? I do not believe we would have had these hard times if it had not been for sin and iniquity. Look at the money that is drank up! The money that is spent for tobacco! That is ruining men—ruining their constitutions. We live in a land flowing with milk and honey. God has blessed this nation; yet men complain of hard times. I tell you there is nothing so extravagant as sin. If a man would seek the kingdom of God first you would not be troubled much about the things of this world. You would not be troubled about your clothing and about what you would eat. That is about all we need. You may have the wealth of this world, but you can't take a penny away with you. You hear it

said that a man died worth millions. The fact is when he dies
he is not worth anything. The wealth that a man may have then
is not of this world. Lay up treasures in heaven, not down here.
You may have millions here and enter eternity a beggar if you
have not become rich toward God.

I remember, a number of years ago, I was working out in the
field. It was before I left home, and I was a little wild in those
days. A man told me something I did not understand; it was a
mystery. We were hoeing corn, and I noticed he was weeping.
Says I, "What is the trouble?" and he went on and told me. It
sounded strange then. I did not understand it. He said when he
left home to make his fortune it was a beautiful morning when
he left his mother's door, and she gave him this text of Scripture:
"Seek first the kingdom of God, and his righteousness; and all
these things shall be added unto you." He said he paid no attention to it. He said there were no railroads in those days, and he
had to walk. He walked from town to town, and the first Sunday
he was away he went into a little country church, and the minister got up and preached from the text, "Seek first the kingdom
of God." He said to himself, "That is my mother's text. I wonder if that man knows me." He thought he was preaching it for
him. But he said to himself that he was not going to seek the
kingdom of God yet; that he was going to get rich, and when he
got rich and was settled down in life he was going to attend to
his soul's interest—just exactly what God told him not to do. He
said the sermon made a deep impression upon him, but that he
had made up his mind that he would not seek God then. He
could not get any work in that town, and he went to another,
and another, and at last he got some work, and he went to church
in the town, and he hadn't been going there a great while before he heard a sermon from the text, "Seek first the kingdom of
God, and his righteousness." He thought God was calling him,
and the sermon and the text made a deep impression on his
mind; but he calmly and deliberately said: "I will not seek the
kingdom of God now, I will wait until I get rich." He said he
finally got through working in that town and he went to another,
and another, and at last he got work in another town. He said he
went to church—he went because his mother had taught him; he

said he didn't feel easy when he stayed away; he said he did not go to get any blessing; just went because he had been educated to go. What was his surprise, he said, when the minister got up in the pulpit and preached from the text, "Seek first the kingdom of God, and his righteousness, and all these things shall be added unto you." He said he thought surely God was calling him; and he said the Spirit strove mightily with him; but he just fought it —made up his mind that he would not become a Christian until he had become settled in life; and he said that all the sermons he heard since made no more of an impression upon him than on that stone, and he struck it with a hoe. It seemed to him as if the Spirit of God had left him. But I could not talk to him. I was a stranger to Christ. But soon after I went off to Boston. When I was converted, almost the first man that came into my mind was that neighbor, and I made up my mind when I went home I would talk with him and tell him about the Saviour. When I got home I made inquiries, and my mother said, "Why, didn't I write you about him?" "Write me what?" "Why, he has gone to the insane asylum, and if any of the neighbors go up to see him he will point his finger at him and will say, 'Young man, seek first the kingdom of God and his righteousness.'" Reason had reeled and tottered from its throne, but the text was still there. God had sent that arrow down into his soul. Long years had rolled away and he could not draw it out of his soul. The next time I went home they told me he was up on his farm, that he was idiotic. I went up to his house, and found him in the rocking chair; he was rocking backwards and forwards, and as I spoke to him he gave me that idiotic look—that vacant look; and I called him by name, and said, "Don't you know me?" He pointed his finger at me and said, "Young man, seek first the kingdom of God and his righteousness." He did not know me—mind all gone, but the text still there. A little while after he died. He lies slumbering in the cemetery where my father is buried; and when I go to visit that cemetery, as I go by that grave, it seems as if I could hear that text coming up from that grave, "Seek first the kingdom of God and his righteousness, and all these things shall be added unto you." My friends, you and I cannot afford to disobey God. We cannot afford to calmly and coolly and deliberately say, "I will not obey." Look around us. Men are snatched away suddenly, and they just pass into eternity. Look at that accident only a few hours ago on the Michigan Central—that night train passing on with great rapidity, and in a moment they passed into eternity.

My friend, if you sleep to-night without seeking the kingdom of God, you are disobeying God. It is a command from God Almighty to every soul here. We have no right to defer it; no right to say that we will seek the kingdom of God to-morrow. To-morrow does not belong to us. To-day—now—is the day of salvation.

You will find in the fifty-fifth chapter of Isaiah, "Seek ye the Lord while he may be found, call ye upon him while he is near." It is not to seek feeling. It is not to seek a sentiment, nor some dogma, nor some creed, but it is to seek the Lord Himself. "Seek ye the Lord while he may be found, call ye upon him while he is near." That is the exhortation. God exhorts you to seek Him while He may be found.

Some one may ask, "How seek Him?" Seek Him with your heart, not with your head. The trouble with a great many is, they seek Him with their head, and they never find Him. It is not a new head, but a new heart, we want. What do you mean by seeking God with your heart? I will tell you: When a man goes into a thing with his heart you can soon tell it. He will be in earnest. Go into the gold regions, and you will find that the miners down in the mines have their hearts there. They are terribly in earnest. Go learn a lesson of the world. See how men seek for wealth! Look at these politicians over the State of Ohio. They can hardly wait until the Sabbath rolls away to begin their work to-morrow. We want men to seek their soul's salvation as they seek for wealth. There is one thing that the Lord hates, and that is half-heartedness. No man ever found God with half a heart.

I said to a man some time ago, "I will tell you when you will be converted. I can tell you the day and the hour." "Well, I would like to have you. I didn't know that you were a prophet." "Well," says I, "I am not a prophet, but I can tell you when you will be converted." "I would like to have you." "Well," says I, when you search for God with all your heart you will find him, and not before." O, my friends, if God is worth having He is worth seeking for with all our hearts, and when men seek Him with all their heart they find Him.

I am tired of hearing people talk about not having any objection to being saved. I said to a man some time ago, "Are you a Christian?" "No." "Well, wouldn't you like to be?" "Well," said he, "I have no objection." "Well," said I, "you will never find Him with that spirit. God never adopts men with that spirit." I tell you that if we are going to get into the kingdom of God we have got to be in earnest.

I read an account some time ago of a vessel being wrecked at sea, and there were not enough life boats for all on board of the vessel, and some were swimming around in the water trying to get into life boats, and one man with a great effort swam to a boat and reached out his right hand. They said they did not dare to take any more in. They begged him to let go but he would not. You know how a drowning man will grasp at a straw. A man took a sword and cut off the man's hand, and the man swam up a second time and he laid hold of that boat with his left hand and they cut off the left hand; and with both hands cut off he swam up to that boat again and seized it with his teeth. It touched their hearts. They could not cut his head off and they drew him into the boat. He saved his life because he was in earnest. If it is the right hand, off with it; if it is the right eye, out with it. The kingdom of God is worth more than all the world. O, may God wake us up to-day, and show us the importance of seeking the kingdom of God with all our hearts.

Now I want to ask this audience one question: Do you believe that the Lord can be found here to-day? Do you believe that a sinner, a man that has been at enmity with God for twenty years, can come in here to-day and find the Lord precious to his soul? Do you believe that? Do you men believe that? Do you ministers believe it? If men will seek Him with all their hearts they can find Him before they go out of this building. Do you believe that? Do you believe you can get eternal life and live with God forever by just seeking for it? You profess to believe it, but you do not believe it. If you did you would seek for it. If Jehovah should send Gabriel down here to say to any one in this building that you might have any one thing you asked for, I venture to say there would be only one cry—a cry that would ring through the building. "Eternal life!" Everything else would fly into the dim past. You would not ask for money. If there was only one thing to ask for, you would ask for eternal life. It is a great thing to live forever. There is not anything to be compared with eternal life. Now, if eternal life can be found here to-day by asking for it, would you not advise every man, woman and child in this house to seek the kingdom of God? Oh! My friends, seek ye the Lord! He has been seeking for you these many years. Seek Him with your heart, and you will find Him.

WEIGHED IN THE BALANCE

DANIEL 5:27

Preface

As EVERYONE KNOWS who is at all acquainted with the literature of Mr. Moody's sermons, he was especially fond of the book of Daniel. Indeed in his *Bible Characters,* there are seven different sermons alone from the book of Daniel. This particular sermon, "Weighed in the Balance," does not relate so much to Daniel's experiences as to the development of the significance of one single word in this fifth chapter, the word *tekel.* What Mr. Moody does here is to take this idea of "weighed in the balance" and use it as an indictment of mankind in general as he is tested by his obedience to the Ten Commandments of the Mosaic decalogue. This theme he developed with greater detail in an entire series of sermons on the Ten Commandments, *Weighed and Wanting,* published in 1898.

I have often wondered where Mr. Moody picked up this word *cavil* which he introduces at the beginning of the second paragraph, "Now you may cavil at the Word of God." Actually, this word appears in the very first line of the sermon published by Mr. Pell.

As far as I recall, this is the only sermon that ends with a dialogue of Mr. Moody and someone sitting in the front row. Pointing to one in his audience, he asked, "My friend, are you tonight ready to be weighed?" When the answer was in the affirmative, Mr. Moody asked, "Have you got Christ?" And the answer was again in the affirmative, which led Mr. Moody to his final invitation.

The text which is here used is from the volume, *Great Joy,* pp. 329-39. The sermon was also printed in *Gospel Awakening* (1879), pp. 471-78; *Great Redemption* (1889), pp. 152-70; *The Old Gospel and Other Addresses* (1882), pp. 100-15; *Sermons, Addresses, and Prayers* (1877), pp. 420-28; and *Dwight L. Moody* (1900), pp. 455-62.

Weighed in the Balance

YOU WILL FIND my text to-night in one short word, "Tekel,"
meaning: "Thou art weighed in the balance and art found wanting." In the fifth chapter of Daniel we read the history of the
King Belshazzar. It is very short. Only one chapter tells us all
we know about him. One short night of his career is all we
see. He just seems to burst upon the stage and then disappears.
We are told that he gave a great feast, and at this feast he had
1,000 of his lords, and they were drinking and praising the gods
of silver, of gold, of brass, of iron, and of wood, out of the vessels which had been brought from the temple at Jerusalem. As
they were drinking out of these vessels of gold and silver from
the house of God—I don't know but what it was at the midnight
hour, all at once came forth the fingers of a man's hand and
began to write upon the wall of the hall. The king turns deathly
pale, his knees shake together, and he trembles from head to
foot. Perhaps if some one had told him the time was coming
when he would be put into the balance and weighed he would
have laughed at him. But he knows the vital hour has come, and
that hand has written his doom in the words "Mene, mene, tekel,
upharsin." He calls the wise men of his kingdom, and the man
who can interpret this will be made the third ruler of his kingdom, and be clothed in scarlet, and have a chain about his neck.
One after another tried, but no uncircumcised eye could make
it out. He was greatly troubled. At last one was spoken of who
had been able to interpret the dream of his father Nebuchadnezzar. He was told if he would send for Daniel he might interpret
the writing. And now the prophet came in and looked upon the
handwriting, and told him how his father had gone against God,
and how he, Belshazzar, had gone against the Lord of Heaven,
and how his reign was finished. And this was the writing: "Mene:
God hath numbered thy kingdom, and finished it; tekel: Thou
art weighed in the balances, and art found wanting; peres: Thy
kingdom is divided, and given to the Medes and Persians. The
trial is over, the verdict is rendered, and the sentence brought
out. That very night the king was hurled from his throne. That
very night the army of Darius came tearing down the streets, and
you might have heard the clash of arms, shouts of war, and have

seen the king's blood mingling with the wine in that banquet hall.

Now I want to call your attention to that word "tekel." We are weighed in the balance. Now you cavil at the word of God; you make light when all is going well in the hour of your prosperity. But when the time of trial comes, and we are called into judgment, it will be altogether different. Suppose the sentence should come down from heaven upon every man and woman in this tabernacle to be weighed in the balance to-night, how would it be with you? Come, my friends, are you ready to be weighed to-night? Not in our own scales, but in God's balance. Suppose the scales were dropped now from the kingdom of God; are you ready to step into the balance and be weighed? Are you willing to be weighed by the law? I can imagine some of you saying, "I wouldn't be weighed by that law (meaning the decalogue) ; I don't believe it." Some men think we are away beyond the Mosaic law; we have got out of it. Why, Christ said in the fifth chapter of Matthew: "Think not that I am come to destroy the law, or the prophets; I am not come to destroy, but to fulfil. Heaven and earth may pass away, but my law shall never pass away"; but not until heaven and earth shall be removed will the word of God be removed. Now the commandments that I read to you to-night are as binding as ever they have been. Many men say that we have no need of the commandments, only the sermon on the Mount. "Think not that I am come to destroy the law, or the prophets: I am not come to destroy, but to fulfil." Now, my friends, are you ready to be weighed by the law of God—by that magic law? What is the first commandment? "Thou shalt have no other gods before me." Are you ready to be weighed by this commandment? Now, the question is, have you fulfilled, or are you ready to fulfil, all the requirements of this law? A great many people say if they keep the commandments they don't need Christ. But have you kept them? I will admit if you keep the commandments you can be saved by them, but is there a man in this audience who can truly say that he has done this? Young lady, can you say: "I am ready to be weighed by the law tonight?" Can you, young man? Now, suppose we have these commandments written upon pieces of iron. You know when you go into a grocery store you see them taking a weight and putting it into the scales against what you have bought. Now, suppose the pieces of iron as weights and the law of God written on them. Take this first commandment, "Thou shalt have no other gods before me" upon one of the weights. Put it in one of the scales and just step on the other. "Thou art weighed in the balance." Is your heart set upon God to-night? Have you no other idol? Do you love Him above father or mother, the wife of your bosom, your children, home or land, wealth or pleasure? Have you got another god before Him? If you have, surely you are not ready to step in and be weighed against that commandment, "Thou shalt have no other god before me." That is the commandment of God, and it is binding to-night. Then take another. You will say there is no trouble about this one. We might go off to other ages or other lands, and we can find people who worship idols, but we have none here. But how many idols have we in our hearts? Many a man says, "Give me money and I will give you heaven; what care I for all the glories and treasures of heaven; give me treasures here. I don't care for heaven. I want to be a successful business man." They make money and business their god. Although they don't make gods of silver and gold, they bow before them. There are more men who worship silver and gold in Chicago than any other god. But take another one: "Thou shalt not take the name of the Lord thy God in vain." Is there a swearing man ready to put the weight into the scales and step in? Young man, have you been taking the name of the Lord in vain to-day? What does he say? "The Lord will not hold him guiltless that taketh his name in vain." I don't believe men would ever have been guilty of swearing unless God had told them not to. They don't swear by their friends, by their fathers and mothers, by their wives, by their children. But because God has forbidden it, man wants to show how he despises His law. "Thou shalt not take the name of the Lord thy God in vain." Blasphemer, go into the scales, and see how quick you will fly out. You will be like a feather in the balance. A great many men think there is nothing very serious in swearing; they don't think there's much wrong in it. Bear in mind that He sees something in it when He says:

"Thou shalt not take the name of the Lord thy God in vain."
You cannot trifle with God. Some men say they never swear
except when they get angry. Suppose you swear only once in six
months, or a year—suppose you swear once in ten years, do you
think God will hold you guiltless for that one act? A man that
swears once shows that his heart is rebellious to God. What are
you going to do, blasphemer? If the balances were here to-night,
and God told you to step in, what would you do?

But take the fourth commandment: "Remember the Sabbath
day to keep it holy." Suppose you could see the law written over
those walls, "Remember the Sabbath day to keep it holy," could
you say that you had observed it? Are you ready to be weighed by
the weight, "Remember the Sabbath day to keep it holy"? Some
of us may be professed Christians, but do we observe the Sabbath? If this country falls into neglect of the observance of the
Sabbath, it will go the way of France, Mexico and Spain. Every
nation that gives up the Sabbath must go down. It is only a
question of time with them. Look when the children of Israel
refused to obey the injunctions of the Lord in regard to the culti-
vation of their land, how He took them into bondage and kept
them for seventy years to let them know that God's land was not
to be trampled under their feet. Are you guilty or not guilty or
innocent in regard to this law: "Thou shalt keep the Sabbath day
holy"? When I was in France in 1867, I could not tell one day
from another. On Sunday stores were open, buildings were being
erected, the same as on other days. See how quick that country
went down. Only a few years ago it stood breast to breast with
other nations, it stood side by side almost with England. But it
didn't have any respect for the Sabbath: it trampled God's message under foot, and when the hour of battle came, God left
them alone. My friends, every nation that tramples the Sabbath
under its feet must go to ruin. Are you innocent or guilty? Do
you keep the Sabbath day holy or not? I have been talking to
those car conductors—and if there's any class of men I pity more
than another it is them—and they have to work on the Sabbath.
Some of you are breaking this law by coming down here on Sunday in the cars. What will you do? Foot it. It will be better for
you. I make a point of never allowing myself to break the Sab-

bath of any man. When I was in London, and it's a pretty big city, you know, in my ignorance I made arrangements to preach four times at different places one Sunday. After I had made the appointments I found I had to walk sixteen miles, and I walked it, and I slept that night with a clear conscience. I want no hackman to rise up in judgment against me. My friends, if we want to help the Sabbath, let business men and Christians never patronize cars on the Sabbath. I would hate to own stock in those horse-car companies, to be the means of taking the Sabbath from these men, and have to answer for it at the day of judgment. No man can work seven days a week and save his soul. And the very best thing we have is being taken from these men by us Christians. Are you willing to step into the balance and be weighed against "Thou shalt keep the Sabbath day holy"?

Well, there is the fifth: "Honor thy father and mother." Are you ready to be weighed against this? Have you honored them? Is there anyone here to-night who is dishonoring father or mother? Now, I've lived nearly forty years, and I've learned one thing if I've learned nothing else, that no man or woman who treats disrespectfully father or mother ever prospers. How many young ladies have married against their father's wishes, and gone off and just made their own ruin. I never knew one case that did not turn out bad. They brought ruin upon themselves. This is a commandment from heaven: "Honor thy father and mother." In the last days men shall be disobedient to parents, void of natural affection; and it seems as if we were living in those days now. How many sons treat their mothers with contempt, make light of their entreaties. God says, "Honor thy father and mother." If the balances were placed in this hall would you be ready to step into them against this commandment? You may make light of it and laugh at it, but young men, remember that God will hedge your way. No man shall succeed that disobeys His commandment. But bear in mind you are not going to be weighed only against this solitary commandment—every weight will be put in.

"Thou shalt not kill." Most of you say, "That don't touch me at all; I never killed anyone; I'm no murderer." Look at that sermon on the Mount, which men think so much of. Look at it. Did you never in your heart wish a man dead who had done you an injury? That's murder. How are you? Innocent or guilty? If you have, you are a murderer at heart. Now, come, my friends, are you ready to be weighed against the law? Ah, if most of us were weighed to-night we would find this word written against us: "Tekel," thou art weighed in the balance and found wanting.

But, let us take another, "Thou shalt not commit adultery." I don't know any sin that afflicts us like this. It is a very delicate subject to approach, but I never preach without being com- pelled to touch upon it. Young men among us are being bound hand and foot with this evil. Young men, hear this law to-night: "Thou shalt not commit adultery." Are you guilty even in thought? How many would come into the Tabernacle but that they are tied hand and foot, as one has been in the halls of vice, and some harlot, whose feet are fastened in hell, clings to him and says: "If you give me up, I will expose you." Can you step on the scales and take that harlot with you? "Thou shalt not com- mit adultery." You may think that no one knows your doings; you may think that they are all concealed; but God knows it. He that covers his sins shall not prosper. Out with it to-night. Con- fess it to your God. Ask Him to snap the fetters that bind you to this sin; ask Him to give you victory over your passions, and shake yourself like Samson and say, "By the grace of God I will not go down to hell with a harlot," and God will give you power. "Thou shalt not commit adultery." As I said the other night, I don't know a quicker way to hell. How many men have by their lecherous life broken their mothers' heart and gone down to their grave rotten, leaving the effect of their sin to their posterity?

Well, let us take up the next. "Thou shalt not steal." How many have been stealing to-day! I may be speaking to some clerk, who perhaps to-day took five cents out of his employer's drawer to buy a cigar, perhaps he took ten cents to get a shave, and thinks he will put it back tomorrow; no one will ever know it. If you have taken a penny you are a thief. Do you ever think how those little stealings may bring you to ruin? Let an employer find it out. If he don't take you into the courts, he will discharge you. Your hopes will be blasted, and it will be hard work to get up again. Whatever condition you are in, do not take a cent that does not belong to you. Rather than steal go up to heaven in poverty—go up to heaven from the poor house—and be honest rather than go through the world in a gilded chariot of stolen riches. A man who takes money that does not belong to him never gets any comfort. He never has any pleasure, for he has a guilty conscience. "Thou shalt not steal." Are you ready to be weighed tonight in the balances?

Then let us take the ninth commandment: "Thou shalt not bear false witness against thy neighbor," or, in other words, thou shalt not be guilty of lying. If you had a chance to make $200 or $300 are you not willing to go into a court and lie to get it? "Thou shalt not bear false witness against thy neighbor." Are you ready to step into the balances against this? Then take another. "Thou shalt not covet thy neighbor's goods." Are you innocent or guilty? How many times I used to covet that which belonged to other people before I was converted. I believe that is one of the greatest sins among us. My friends, how is it? Innocent or guilty? But suppose you are innocent of all these ten commandments, let us take that eleventh commandment of Christ's: "A new commandment I give unto you; thou shalt love one another." My friends, how is it to-night? Is love reigning in your hearts? Do you love your neighbors? Do you try to do them good, or are you living a life of selfishness, merely for yourself.

Now I can imagine that nearly every man or woman is saying to himself or herself, "If we are to be judged by these laws how are we going to be saved?" Every one of them has been broken by all people. The moral man is just as guilty as the rest. There is not a moralist in Chicago who, if he steps into those scales, can be saved; "except a man be born again, he cannot see the kingdom of God." "Except ye repent ye shall all perish." That is on one side of the scales, and He will see on the other, "Except ye be converted ye shall not enter the kingdom of God." I have heard a good many pharisees saying, "These meetings are reaching the drunkards and gamblers and harlots; they are doing good"; but they don't think they need these meetings. They are all right; they are moral men. "Except a man be born again, he cannot see the kingdom of God." I don't care how moral he is. Nicodemus was probably one of the most moral men of his day.

He was a teacher of the law; yet Christ said: "Except a man be born again, he cannot see the kingdom of God." I would a good deal rather preach to thieves and drunkards and vagabonds, than preach to self-righteous pharisees. You don't have to preach to those men weeks and months to convince them that they are sinners. When a man learns that he has need of God, and that he is a sinner, it is very easy to reach him. But, my friends, the self-righteous pharisee needs salvation as much as any drunkard that walks the streets of Chicago. There is another class I want to speak of. If I had time I would just like to take up the different classes in the city. That class is the rum-sellers. Put the rum-sellers in the balances. They ignore God's laws, but by and by He will say to them, "Tekel," "Woe be to the man that put the bottle to his neighbor's lips." My friends, I would rather have that right hand cut off before I would give the bottle to a man. I would rather have my right arm cut off than deal out death and damnation to my fellow-men. If any poor drunkard here should be summoned into eternity to-night—weighed in the balances, what would he hear? "No drunkard shall inherit the kingdom of God." I can see how he would reel and stagger when he heard that. "No drunkard shall inherit the kingdom of heaven."

My friends, if you don't repent of your sins and ask Him for mercy, there is no hope for you. Let me ask you to-night to take this question home to yourself. If a summons should come at midnight to be weighed in the balances, what will become of your souls, because the law of God must be kept. Now there are many of you only making professions. You belong to the First Methodist Church, or you may be a member of a Baptist Church, but are you ready to be weighed—ready to step into these scales to-night? I think a great many would be found like those five foolish virgins. When the hour came they would be found with no oil in their lamps. If there is a person here to-night who has only an empty lamp, or is living on mere formalism, I beg of you to give it up. Give up that dead, cold, miserable lukewarmness. God will spit it out of His mouth. He will have none of it. Wake up. Some of you have gone almost to sleep while I have been trying to weigh you in the balances. God will weigh you, and then if you have not Christ it will be "Tekel."

I can imagine some of you saying: "I would just like Moody to put those tests to himself. I wonder what would become of him." My dear friends, if God was to ask me to-night I would tell Him "I am ready." I don't say this in any spirit of egotism, of self-righteousness, remember. If you ask me if I have broken the law of Moses, I would answer "Yes, sir." Ask me if I have broken the commandments: "Yes, sir." You may ask me then how I am ready to be weighed. If I step into the scales to-night the Son of God will step into the scales with me. I would not dare to go into them without Him. If I did, how quick the scales would go up. If a man has not got Christ, when the hour comes for him to be weighed, it will be "Tekel, tekel, tekel." How are you to-night, my friend—ready to be weighed? (pointing to one of the audience) .

Answer—Yes, sir.

Mr. Moody—Have you got Christ?

Answer—Yes, sir.

Mr. Moody—That's right. Suppose I put the question to every man and woman in this audience. How quick many of them would begin to color up. Oh, my friends, if you haven't got Him, get Him to-night. May God open your eyes and your minds to receive Him before you leave this Tabernacle to-night. Christ kept the law; Christ was the end of the law. If He had broken the law He would have had to die for Himself; but He kept it, and we are enabled to be clothed in righteousness. My friends, it is the height of madness to go out of this hall to-night and run the risk of being called by God and have to answer without Him. Now is the day and hour to accept salvation, and then He will be with us. Then there will be no alarm with us. I pity those Christian people who are afraid of death. They need not be afraid of death if they have Him. When He is with us it is only a translation. We are absent from the body to be present with the Lord. Here is the gospel of Jesus Christ. Will you be saved to-night? If you do not, when by and by God summons you into these scales, it will be written over you: "Tekel, tekel; thou art weighed in the balances and art found wanting." My friends, what will you do to-night? Remain as you are and be lost, or accept salvation and be saved? Let us pray.

EXCUSES

Preface

I DO NOT KNOW of any printed sermon of Mr. Moody's in which he more closely kept to the theme announced than he does here. The word *excuse,* in noun and verbal form, occurs over thirty times! I find fourteen illustrations here, two of them of such great length that they themselves compose about one-fourth of the entire sermon. This is the only place that I can recall Mr. Moody making the statement, "I have missed a good many appointments in my life." Though in many sermons Mr. Moody often introduces illustrations with the words, "I remember," he does so in this sermon with even greater frequency.

In spite of the fact that Mr. Moody never allows his audience to forget that he is talking about "excuses," for some strange reason the last illustration with which the sermon closes—and a long one and a good one it is—has nothing whatever to do with excuses. Probably Mr. Moody had not intended to introduce this illustration when he was planning the sermon.

This sermon is in *Great Joy* (1879), pp. 118-33; *Great Redemption* (1889), pp. 101-21; *Sermons, Addresses, and Prayers* (1877), pp. 189-202; *Select Sermons* (1881), pp. 97-127 (two sermons); *Addresses by D. L. Moody;* and *Popular Present-Day Excuses* (London, 1875), pp. 87-107; and in Charles F. Goss, *Echoes from the Pulpit and Platform,* pp. 384-98.

The Sinner's Excuses Swept Away

LUKE 14:19: "I pray thee have me excused."

CHRIST HAD BEEN INVITED TO DINE with a rich Pharisee, and it seemed as though this man had gathered his friends together in a kind of conspiracy to catch Christ. They watched Him. A man who had had dropsy was placed before Jesus, as though they wanted to see what He would do. Christ read their hearts, and so before He healed the man He asked them if it was lawful to heal on the Sabbath day. But they didn't want to answer, for fear they'd betray themselves, and so they held their peace. Then Christ put the question to them in another way, and asked them if any of them had an ox or an ass fall into a pit, should he not straightway pull him out on the Sabbath day, and then he healed the man, as the Pharisees and lawyers weren't able to answer Him. Then he told them about the feast, and told them to be humble. When a man prepares a feast, men rush in; but when God prepares one they all begin to make excuses, and don't want to go. The first excuse was that made by Adam, "The woman thou gavest me, she gave me to eat." These men that excused themselves made manufactured excuses; they didn't really have any. The drunkard, the libertine, the business man, the citizen, the harlot, all had their excuses. If God were to take men at their word about these excuses, and swept every one into his grave who had an excuse, there would be a very small congregation in the Tabernacle next Sunday, there would be little business in Chicago, and in a few weeks the grass would be growing on these busy streets. Every man who was nursing a sin had an excuse, as though God had asked them to go into a plague-stricken city, or a hospital, or to hear a dry lecture, or something repelling and objectionable, something that wasn't for their greatest good.

Take the excuses. There wasn't one that wasn't a lie. The devil made them all; and if the sinner hadn't one already, the devil was there at his elbow to suggest one, about the truth of the Bible, or something of that sort. One of the excuses mentioned was that the man invited had bought a piece of ground, and had to look at it. Real estate and corner lots were keeping a good many men out of God's kingdom. It was a lie to say that he had to go and see it then, for he ought to have looked at it before he bought it. Then the next man said he'd bought some oxen, and must prove them. That was another lie; for if he hadn't proved them before he bought them he ought to have done, and could have done, it after the supper just as well as before it. But the third man had the silliest, the worst excuse of all; he said he had married a wife, and couldn't come. Why didn't he bring her with him? She would have liked the supper just as well as he, and would have enjoyed a supper, as almost any young bride would.

These seemed to be foolish excuses, but they were not any more so than the excuses of to-day. Indeed, the excuses of men are getting worse and worse all the time. They say they can't believe the Bible; it's so mysterious. Well, what of it? Infidels, skeptics, pantheists, deists, said they didn't believe the Bible. Had they ever used it? Did they read it as carefully as they read any other book? This was their excuse. If everybody could understand everything the Bible said, it wouldn't be God's book; if Christians, if theologians had studied it for forty, fifty, sixty years, and then only began to understand it, how could a man expect to understand it by one reading? A child the first day at school couldn't even know the alphabet, and yet it wasn't a sign that it was a poor school because he didn't learn the first day all about grammar, arithmetic, and geometry. Another said God was a hard Master. No; that was one of Satan's lies. The devil's the hard master. In the Tombs in New York there is over the door the remark, "The way of the transgressor is hard." God's yoke is easy, His burden light. Ask prisoners, ask gamblers, ask sinners, if Satan's yoke is easy. It's the hardest of all. God's service a hard one! How will that sound in the judgment? Many said it wasn't that, but there is such a struggle. Wasn't all life a struggle? Some said they were wicked. Those are just the kind Jesus came to save. They weren't too wicked to be saved. They were so worldly-minded, so hard-hearted; that was another falsehood. Look at what God did for Bunyan and John Newton and many others who were the wickedest, and even the thief on the cross. God is already reconciled; He doesn't need the sinner to be reconciled to Him. The Lord prepares the sinner.

Yet you hear people say they can't understand that; they cannot imagine but *they* have to do something to satisfy God. But I tell you that God is satisfied, God is reconciled. You have the word of Paul that God is reconciled to us. Yes, thank God, He is reconciled to the world. Can *you* reconcile God? Christ has done that. The moment a sinner takes this to heart, and comes to Jesus, that moment he is saved. Perhaps a story will illustrate this as well as anything. In England I was told about an only son—these only sons are hard to bring up properly; they have every whim and caprice gratified; they generally grow up headstrong, self-willed, and obstinate, and make it miserable for any one to have anything to do with them. Well, this son had a father something like himself in disposition. And one day a quarrel arose between them, and at last, as the son would not give in and own he was wrong, the father, in a fit of anger, said that he wished his son would leave his house and never come back again. "Well," rejoined the boy (as angry as his father), "I will leave, and I never will enter your house again until you ask me." "Well, then, you won't come back in a hurry," replied his father. The boy then left. The father gave up the boy, but the mother did not. Perhaps these men here won't understand that, but you women do. A great many things will separate a man from his wife, a father from his son, but nothing in the wide, wide world will ever separate a mother from her child. A jury can bring in a verdict against her son; the hisses may go up against him; he is condemned to be hanged; there is not a friendly paper to write an article in his favor. But if his mother be there, the boy has at least one eye to rest upon him, one heart to beat in sympathy with him. He is taken to the cold, damp cell and left to his fate. All forsake him but his mother. She comes there; she puts her arms around his neck; she kisses him; she would spend all the time with him if the officers would allow it. She cannot save him. The day before his execution she sees him for the last time; she has not the courage to see him in the shadow of the gallows. The supreme moment at length arrives; he is led forth, and in a few moments he dangles a corpse. Does the mother then forget him? No; even now she goes to his grave, strews flowers upon it, and waters them with her tears. A mother's love is next to God's love. Death is stronger than everything else; yes, but with the exception of one thing—a mother's love. Death and decay may wreck this city, buildings may cease to exist, everything yields before them but a mother's love. To refer to the illustration again: When the father had given the boy up, he thought he would never come back. The mother was taken very sick. She had been trying by every means in her power to effect a reconciliation between the father and son. When she found she could not recover from her illness she again renewed her efforts with all the power of a mother's love. She wrote to her son, imploring him to ask his father's forgiveness. He sent word back that he would not write to his father unless his father first wrote to him. "I will never come home until he asks me," he said. The mother began to get lower and lower. Her husband at this time came to the bedside and asked if there was anything he could do for her. "Yes, yes," she cried, "there is one thing— you can send for my boy. That is the only wish I have on earth that is not gratified. If you do not care for him while I am alive, who will care for him when I am gone? I cannot bear to die and leave my child among strangers. Just let me see him and speak to him and I will die in peace." The father said he could not send for him. He could, but he wouldn't. He did not want to. The mother has but a few hours now to live. She again beseeches her husband that he will send for their son. The father said he would send a dispatch to him, but in her name. "No, no; that would not do." Well, he can stand it no longer, and he signs his own name at the foot of the telegram. It was sent, and the moment the boy received it he took the first train home. The father was standing by the side of the bed when the son arrived. But when he saw the door open he turned his back upon him and walked away. The mother grasped the hand of her boy and pressed it again and again, and kissed him fervently. "Oh! Just speak to your father, won't you? Just speak the first word." "No, mother, I will not speak to him until he speaks to me." The excitement was too much and she was rapidly sinking. She told her husband she was dying. She now took his hand in hers, and held the hand of her boy in the other, and sought and strove to bring about a reconciliation. But neither would speak. With her last strength she then placed the hand of the son into the hand of the father and sank down into the arms of death, and was borne by the angels into the kingdom of God. The father looked at the wife and then at the boy, he caught his eye; they fell upon each other's necks, and there stood weeping by the bed of the departed. That is the illustration I have given, but it is not a fair illustration in this respect: God is not angry with us. With that exception it is a good illustration of reconciliation. Christ brought the hand of the Father clear down to the world; He put the hand of the sinner into the hand of His Father and died that they might be reconciled. You have nothing to do then to bring about a reconciliation. God is already reconciled to us and is ready to save us. "Blessed is he who shall be at the marriage supper of the Lamb." I have missed a good many appointments in my life, but there is one I will not miss. I would rather be at the marriage feast than have the whole world rolled at my feet. I want to be there and sit down with Isaac and Jacob and Abraham, at that supper. It is an invitation for joy and gladness that comes from the King of kings, from the Lord of glory, to every man and woman in this assembly—the invitation to be at the marriage supper of the Lamb. It is not a personal invitation, but a universal one—"Go out into the highways and hedges and compel them to come in, that my house may be filled." Bid them come, "the poor and the maimed, and the halt, and the blind," to the marriage feast prepared at great expense by our blessed Redeemer.

People began to make excuses very early in the history of Christianity, and they are still at it. Nineteen hundred years have nearly rolled away, and still there are excuses. One of the excuses that we very often hear people giving is, that they don't want to become Christians because it will make them gloomy— they will have to put on long faces and button their coats up, cut off all joy and walk through the world till they get to Heaven, where they will have pleasure forevermore. We look forward to that happy future, but, thank God, we have some pleasure here; indeed, no man in the world should be so happy as a man of

God. It is one continual source of gladness. He can look up and say, "God is my Father," "Christ is my Saviour," and "the Church is my mother." All who think otherwise than that a Christian life is one of unceasing joy are deceiving themselves. I was going by a saloon the other day and saw a sign, "Drink and be merry." Poor, blind, deluded fellows, if they think this will make them merry. If you want to be merry, you must come to the living fountain that bursts from the throne of God; then you will have true pleasure. A man away from God cannot have true pleasure. He is continually thirsting for something he cannot get—thirsting for something that can quench his thirst—he cannot get it until he comes to the living fountain. My friends, that is just another wile of the devil to keep men from grace. It is false. The more a man is lifted up to Heaven, the more joy and peace and gladness he has. He is lifted away from gloom. Look at a man on his way to execution. Suppose I ran up to him, holding out my hand and saying: "There is a pardon that has been signed by the Governor," and I give it to him. Would he be gloomy and joyless? That is Christ. He comes down with a pardon to us poor men and women, on our way to execution. Yonder is a man starving. I go to him and give him bread. Is that going to make him gloomy? A poor man comes along crying with thirst, and I give him a glass of ice water; would that make him gloomy? That's what Christ is doing for us. He has a well of living water, and He asks every thirsty soul to drink freely. Don't you believe for a moment that Christianity is going to make you gloomy.

I remember when I was a boy I thought I would wait till I died and then become a Christian. I thought if I had the consumption, or some lingering disease, I would have plenty of time to become one, and in the meantime I would enjoy the best of the pleasures of the world. My friends, I was at that time under the power of the devil. The idea that a man has more pleasure away from church is one of the devil's lies. Do not believe it, but accept of this universal invitation to the marriage feast.

I can imagine some men saying, "Mr. Moody has not touched my case at all. That is not the reason why I won't accept Christ. I don't know if I am one of the elect." How often am I met with this excuse—how often do I hear it in the inquiry-room! How many men fold their arms and say, "If I am one of the elect I will be saved; and if I ain't, I won't. No use of your bothering about it." Why don't some of these merchants say, "If God intends to make me a successful merchant in Chicago, I will be one whether I like it or not; and if He doesn't, I won't." If you are sick, if a doctor prescribes for you, don't take the medicine; throw it out of the door; it don't matter, for if God has decreed you are going to die, you will; and if He hasn't, you will get better. If you use that argument you may as well not walk home from this Tabernacle. If God has said you'll get home, you'll get there—you'll fly through the air, if you have been elected to go home. These illustrations are just the same as the excuse. You cannot go up there and give that excuse. The water of life is offered freely to every one. No unconverted man in the wide, wide world has anything to do with the doctrine of election any more than I have to do with the government of China. That epistle of Paul was written to godly men. Suppose I pick up a letter and open it, and it tells me about the death of my wife. Dear me—my wife dead. But I look on the other side of the letter and find that it is directed to another man. And so a great many people take Paul's letter to the churches and take it as a personal letter. This is what you have to take up: "Whosoever will, let him drink of the water of life freely." He came down sixty years after His resurrection and said to John, put it so broad that no one will mistake it—put it so broad that no one in Chicago can be stumbling over it—so that all men may see it plainly—"Whosoever will, let him drink of the water of life freely." If you will, you will; if you won't, you won't. Do you think that God would come down here to give you salvation without giving you the power to take it, and then condemn you to eternity for not taking it? With the gift comes the power, and you can take it and live if you will. Don't stumble over election any more. You have to deal with that broad proclamation: "Whosoever will, let him drink of the waters of life freely." I can imagine some one in the gallery clear up there saying, "I never have bothered my head about election; I don't believe men are gloomy when they become Christians. If I was alone I would tell you my reason, but I do not like to get up in this large assemblage and talk here. The fact is, there are hypocrites in the churches. I know a man, a prominent man in the church, who cheated me out of twenty-five dollars. I won't accept this invitation because of those hypocrites in the churches." My friend, you will find very few there if you get to Heaven. There won't be a hypocrite in the next world, and if you don't want to be associated with hypocrites in the next world, you will take this invitation. Why, you will find hypocrites everywhere. One of the apostles was himself the very prince of hypocrites, but he didn't get to Heaven. You will find plenty of hypocrites in the church. They have been there for the last eighteen hundred years, and will probably remain there. But what is that to you? This is an individual matter between you and your God. Is it because there are hypocrites you are not going to accept the invitation?

"Ah, well, Mr. Moody, that is not my case. I am a business man, and I have no time. Since the Chicago fire I have had as much as I could attend to in recovering what I lost." If I stood at the door and asked any one who went out to accept the invitation, I believe hundreds of you would say, "Mr. Moody, you will have to excuse me to-night; time is very precious with me, and you'll have to excuse me." What have you been doing the last twenty, thirty, forty, fifty years that you haven't had a moment to devote to the acceptance of this invitation? That is the cry of the world to-day: "Time is precious; business must be attended to, and we have no time to spare." Some of you women will say, "I cannot wait; I have to go home and put the children to bed; this is more important." My friends, to accept this invitation is more important than anything else in this world. There is nothing in the world that is so important as the question of accepting the invitation. How many mechanics in this building have spent five years learning your trade, in order to support your families and support yourselves a few years—forty or fifty years at the longest? How many professional men have toiled and worked hard for years to get an education that they might go out to the world and cope with it, and during all these years have not had a minute to seek their salvation? Is that a legitimate excuse? Tell Him to-night that you haven't time, or let this be the night—the hour —cost you what it will, when you shall say, "By the grace of God

I will accept the invitation and press up to the marriage supper of the Lamb."

"Oh, but that is not my case," says another. "I have time. If I thought I could become a Christian I would sit here all night and let business and everything else go, and press into the kingdom of God. I am not fit to become a Christian; that's the trouble with me." He says: "Go into the highways and hedges," and "bring in hither the poor, and the maimed, and the halt, and the blind"— just invite them all, without distinction of the sect or creed, station or nationality; never mind whether they are rich or poor. If the Lord don't complain about your fitness, you shouldn't look to see if you have the right kind of clothes. I had to notice during the war, when enlisting was going on, sometimes a man would come up with a nice silk hat on, patent-leather boots, nice kid gloves, and a fine suit of clothes, which probably cost him a hundred dollars; perhaps the next man who came along would be a hod-carrier, dressed in the poorest kind of clothes. Both had to strip alike and put on the regimental uniform. So when you come and say you ain't fit, haven't got good clothes, haven't got righteousness enough, remember that He will furnish you with the uniform of Heaven, and you will be set down at the marriage feast of the Lamb. I don't care how black and vile your heart may be, only accept the invitation of Jesus Christ and He will make you fit to sit down with the rest at that feast. How many are continually crying out, "I am too bad; no use of me trying to become a Christian." This is the way the devil works. Sometimes he will say to a man, "You don't want to be saved; you are good enough already"; and he will point to some black-hearted hypocrite and say: "Look at him and see how you appear in comparison; you are far better than he is." But, by and by, the man gets a glimpse of the blackness of his heart, and his conscience troubles him. Then says the devil: "You are too bad to be saved; the Lord won't save such as you; you are too vile; you must get better before you try to get God to save you." And so men try to make themselves better, and instead, get worse all the time. The Gospel bids you come as you are. Seek first the kingdom of Heaven—make no delay; come just as you are. I heard of an artist who wanted to get a man to sit for a painting of the prodigal son. He went down to the almshouses and the prisons, but couldn't get one. Going through the streets one day, he found a poor, wretched man, a beggar, coming along, and he asked him if he would sit for the study. He said he would. A bargain was made and the artist gave him his address. The time for the appointment arrived, and the beggar promptly arrived and said to the artist: "I have come to keep that appointment which I made with you." "An appointment with me?" replied the artist; "you are mistaken: I have an appointment with a beggar to-day." "Well," said the man, "I am that beggar, but I thought I would put on a new suit of clothes before I came to see you." "I don't want you," was the artist's reply, "I want a beggar." And so a great many people come to God with their self-righteousness, instead of coming in their raggedness. Why, some one has said, "It is only the ragged sinners that open God's wardrobe." If you want to start out to get a pair of shoes from a passer-by, you would start out bare-footed, wouldn't you? I remember a boy to whom I gave a pair of boots, and I found him shortly after in his bare feet again. I asked him what he had done with them, and he replied that when he was dressed up it spoiled his business; when he was dressed up no one would give him anything. By keeping his feet naked he got as many as five pairs of boots a day. So, if you want to come to God, don't dress yourself up. It is the naked sinners God wants to save. Come to Him after you have cast off your self-righteousness and the Son of God will receive you.

I remember, some years ago, of a man who had gone to sea. He led a wild, reckless life. When his mother was alive she was a praying mother. Ah, how many men have been saved by their mothers after they have gone up to Heaven, and perhaps her influence made him think sometimes. When at sea, a desire of leading a better life came over him, and when he got on shore, he thought he would join the Freemasons. He made application, but upon investigation his character proved he was only a drunken sailor, and he was black-balled. He next thought of joining the Odd Fellows, and applied, but his application met with a like result. While he was walking up Fulton street, one day, a little tract was given him—an invitation to the prayer-meeting.

He came and Christ received him. I remember him getting up in the meeting and telling how the Freemasons had black-balled him, how the Odd Fellows had black-balled him, and how Christ had received him as he was. A great many orders and societies will not receive you, but I tell you, He will receive you, vile as you are—He, the Saviour of sinners—He, the Redeemer of the lost world—He bids you come just as you are.

Ah, there is another voice coming down from the gallery yonder: "I have intellectual difficulties; I cannot believe." A man came to me some time ago and said: "I cannot." "Cannot what?" I asked. "Well," said he, "I cannot believe." "Who?" "Well," he repeated, "I cannot believe." "Who?" I asked. "Well-I-can't-believe-myself." "Well, you don't want to." Make yourself out false every time, but believe in the truth of Christ. If a man says to me, "Mr. Moody, you have lied to me; you have dealt falsely with me," it may be so, but no man on the face of the earth can ever say that God ever dealt unfairly, or that He lied to him. If God says a thing, it is true. We don't ask you to believe in any man on the face of the earth, but we ask you to believe in Jesus Christ, who never lied—who never deceived any one. If a man says he cannot believe Him, he says what is untrue.

Ah, but there is another voice coming down from the gallery "I can't feel." That is the very last excuse. When a man comes with this excuse he is getting pretty near the Lord. We are having a body of men in England giving a new translation of the Scriptures. I think we should get them to put in a passage relating to feeling. With some people it is feel, feel, feel all the time. What kind of feeling have you got? Have you got a desire to be saved? Have you got a desire to be present at the marriage supper? Suppose a gentleman asked me to dinner. I say, "I will see how I feel." "Sick?" he might ask. "No; it depends on how I feel." That is not the question—it is whether I will accept the invitation or not. The question with us is, Will we accept salvation—will you believe? There is not a word about feelings in the Scriptures. When you come to your end, and you know that in a few days you will be in the presence of the Judge of all the earth, you will remember this excuse about feelings. You will be saying, "I went up to the Tabernacle, I remember, and I felt very good, and before the meeting was over I felt very bad, and I didn't feel I had the right kind of feeling to accept the invitation." Satan will then say, "I made you feel so." Suppose you build your hopes and fix yourself upon the Rock of Ages, the devil cannot come to you. Stand upon the Word of God and the waves of unbelief cannot touch you; the waves of persecution cannot assail you; the devil and all the fiends of hell cannot approach you if you only build your hopes upon God's Word. Say, "I will trust Him, though He slay me—I will take God at His word."

I haven't exhausted all the excuses. If I had, you would make more before to-morrow morning. What has to be done with all the excuses is to bundle them all up and label them "Satan's lies." There is not an excuse but it is a lie. When you stand at the throne of God no man can give an excuse. If you have got a good excuse, don't give it up for anything I have said; don't give it up for anything your mother may have said; don't give it up for anything your friend may have said. Take it up to the bar of God and state it to Him; but if you have not got a good excuse—an excuse that will stand eternity—let it go to-night, and flee to the arms of a loving Saviour. It is easy enough to excuse yourself to hell, but you cannot excuse yourself to Heaven. If you want an excuse Satan will always find one ready for you. Accept the invitation now, my friends. Let your stores be closed till you accept this invitation; let your households go till you accept this invitation. Do not let the light come, do not eat, do not drink, till you accept the most important thing to you in this wide world. Will you stay to-night and accept this invitation? Don't make light of it. I can imagine some of you saying, "Well, I never get so low as to make light of religion." Suppose I got an invitation to dinner from a citizen of Chicago for to-morrow and I don't answer it; I tear the invitation up. Would not that be making light of it? Suppose you pay no attention to the invitation to-night; is not that making light of it? Would any one here be willing to write out an excuse something like this: "The Tabernacle, October 29. To the King of Heaven: While sitting in the Tabernacle to-day I received a very pressing invitation from one of your servants to sit at the marriage ceremony of the Son of God. I pray you have me excused." Is there a man or woman in this assembly would take their pen and write their name at the bottom of it? Is there a man or woman whose right hand would not forget its cunning, and whose tongue would not cleave to their mouth, if they were trying to do it? Well, you are doing this if you get up and go right out after you have heard the invitation. Who will write this: "To the Lord of lords and King of Glory: While sitting in the Tabernacle this beautiful Sabbath evening, October 29, 1876, I received a pressing invitation from one of your servants to be present at the marriage supper. I hasten to accept." Will any one sign this? Who will put their name to it? Is there not a man or woman saying down deep in their soul, "By the grace of God I will sign it"; "I will sign it by the grace of God, and will meet that sainted mother who has gone there"; "I will sign and accept that invitation and meet that loving wife or dear child." Are there not some here to-night who will accept that invitation?

I remember while preaching in Glasgow an incident occurred which I will relate. I had been preaching there several weeks, and the night was my last one, and I pleaded with them as I had never pleaded there before. I urged those people to meet me in that land. It is a very solemn thing to stand before a vast audience for the last time and think you may never have another chance of asking them to come to Christ. I told them I would not have another opportunity, and urged them to accept, and just asked them to meet me at that marriage supper. At the conclusion I soon saw a tall young lady coming into the inquiry-room. She had scarcely come in when another tall young lady came in, and she went up to the first and put her arms around her and wept. Pretty soon another young lady came and went up to the first two and just put her arms around them both. I went over to see what it was, and found that although they had been sitting in different parts of the building the sure arrow of conviction went down to their souls and brought them to the inquiry-room. Another young lady came down from the gallery and said, "Mr. Moody, I want to become a Christian." I asked a young Christian to talk to her, and when she went home that night, about ten o'clock—her mother was sitting up for her—she said, "Mother, I have accepted the invitation to be present at the marriage supper of the Lamb." Her mother and father lay awake that night talking about the salvation of their child. That was Friday night, and next day (Saturday) she was unwell, and before long her sickness developed into scarlet fever, and a few days after I got this letter:

"Mr. Moody—Dear Sir: It is now my painful duty to intimate to you that the dear girl concerning whom I wrote you on Monday has been taken away from us by death. Her departure, however, has been signally softened to us, for she told us yesterday she was 'going home to be with Jesus,' and after giving messages to many, told us to let Mr. Moody and Mr. Sankey know that she died a happy Christian.

"My dear sir, let us have your prayers that consolation and needed resignation and strength may be continued to us, and that our two dear remaining little ones may be kept in health if our Father wills. I repeated a line of the hymn—

> " 'In the Christian's home in glory,
> There remains a land of rest,—

"When she took it up at once and tried to sing,

> " 'There the Saviour's gone before me,
> To fulfill my soul's request.'

"This was the last conscious thing she said. I should say that my dear girl also expressed a wish that the lady she conversed with on Friday evening should also know that she died a happy Christian."

When I read this I said to Mr. Sankey, "If we do nothing else we have been paid for coming across the Atlantic. There is one soul we have saved, whom we will meet on the resurrection morn."

Oh, my dear friends, are there not some here to-night who will decide this question? Do accept this invitation; let sickness come, let sorrow come, you will be sure of meeting at the marriage supper of the Lamb. Blessed is he who shall be found at that marriage feast.

"SON, REMEMBER"

LUKE 16:25

Preface

ONE WOULD NEVER KNOW from the title that this particular sermon was on the subject of hell unless he knew what was to be found in the text, Luke 16:25. Sometimes Mr. Moody actually entitled his message, "A Sermon About Hell," sometimes simply using the word "Hell" and once, most dramatically, "How Memory Torments the Lost Soul." The sermon used here is from *London Discourses* (1875), pp. 107-16. Sometimes Mr. Moody began his sermon with a more or less lengthy discourse on the subject of "Memory," which was very well developed, and in which he significantly says, "There was just one thing that this man we have read of tonight in this chapter took away with him and that was his memory." Sometimes in preaching this sermon, Mr. Moody would begin, "A man came to me the other day and said, 'I like your preaching. You don't preach hell and I don't suppose you believe in one.'"

Mr. Moody most effectively introduces various characters, such as Cain, the antediluvians, and the citizens of Sodom and Gomorrah, as remembering in hell their antagonism to God, and their crimes. He presses home the fact that in that world there will be no Bible and no comforting loved ones. In most of the copies of this sermon appearing in book form, half of the sermon is devoted to illustrations. On rare occasions, as sometimes in preaching this sermon, Mr. Moody quoted poetry. Other appearances of the sermon are to be found in *Gospel Awakening* (1879), pp. 292-97; *Great Joy* (1879), pp. 230-43; *Glad Tidings* (1876), pp. 252-62; *Moody's Great Sermons* (1899), pp. 230-62 (a very long sermon); E. L. Pell, *Dwight L. Moody* (1900), pp. 498-508; *Sermons, Addresses, and Prayers* (1877), pp. 331-34; and *The Way Home* (1904), pp. 80-93. This is one of those sermons which as early as 1875 appeared as a separate publication, *Son, Remember*. There is a different sermon, "Hell," in *Moody: His Words, Work, and Workers,* W. H. Daniels, ed. (1877), pp. 457-67.

"Son, Remember"

Luke 16:25

IN ANOTHER PLACE of the Scripture we read of the "worm that dieth not" and the "fire that is not quenched." I believe the "worm" spoken of is memory. I believe that is what is going to make hell so terrible to those that have lived in a Gospel land, is to think what they might have been, to think how they might have spent eternity in that world of light.

Now we read in this portion of Scripture that this rich man is in another world. His soul has left the body, he has gone beyond time, and he is now in another world. Some people say that when we preach about hell it is only to terrify the people—only to alarm them. Now I am no alarmist, and if I could terrify any one, and try to scare them into the kingdom of God, I would not. But at the same time, if I am to be a messenger for God, I must tell the whole message—I must not keep back any part of the Word of God. The same Christ that tells us of heaven with all its glories tells us of hell with all its horrors; and no one will accuse Christ of drawing this picture to terrify people, or to alarm them, if it were not true.

This picture is one that He has drawn Himself. I have read some sermons about hell, but I never read one more terrible than this one. I have never seen a picture drawn more fearful than this one that is drawn here, of a rich man "clothed in purple and fine linen," and who "fared sumptuously every day" while he was in this world; but we catch a glimpse of him in another world, and we find him there lifting up his voice in hell, and crying in torment.

Some tell us there is no hell and some that there is no heaven. If I had to give up one, I would have to give up the other. The same Bible that tells us of heaven tells us of hell. The same Saviour that came down from heaven to tell us about heaven, tells us about hell. He speaks about our escaping the damnation of hell, and there is no one that has lived since that could tell us as much about it as Himself. If there is no hell, let us burn our Bibles. Why spend so much time studying the Bible? Why spend so much time and so much money in building churches?

Let us turn our churches into places of commerce or ·of amusement. Let us eat and drink and be merry, for ·we will soon be gone if there is no hereafter. Let us build a monument for Paine and Voltaire. Let us build a tomb over Christianity, and shout over it,

"There is no hell to receive us, there is no God to condemn sin; there is no heaven, there is no hereafter!"

Let us be in earnest. If there *is* a heaven and a hell, then let us act as God would have us act. God was in earnest when He gave Christ to die for us. Christ was in earnest when He went to Calvary and suffered that terrible death—it was to save us from that terrible hell. If I believed there was no hell, you would not find me going from town to town, spending day and night preaching and proclaiming the Gospel, and urging men to escape the damnation of hell. I would take things easy.

Oh, my friends, I cannot but believe it! And if there is any one here in doubt about it, why not be honest? If you believe you have a Creator, why not ask Him to give you light about the future? There was a time when I did not believe it; but God revealed it to me. It is a matter of revelation. It is Satan that is telling us there is no hereafter and no hell, because the Word of God teaches it so plainly. And if there is a hell, we had better find it out before we get there; it is a good deal better for us to find it out here than to be laughing and joking about it. It makes me feel very sad to hear men speaking so flippantly about hell, and making jokes about it. God is not to be trifled with. Think of this man in that lost world crying for one drop of water, and then asking that Abraham might send one to comfort him; but there was a gulf fixed that no man could cross! God has fixed that gulf.

THE TIME OF SEPARATION

The time is coming when there will be a separation. The time is coming when that praying wife and that godless, Christless husband shall be separated. The time is coming when that godly, sainted mother will be lifted up to heaven, and that scorning, infidel son will be cast down to hell unless he is wise and accepts of salvation.

Now the thought I want to bring out is just this—that there is

Memory in Hell

What did Abraham say to this man? "Son, remember." Oh, may this text be engraved on your heart!

"Son, remember." God wants you to wake up and remember before it is too late. It is a good deal better for a man to be wise, and stop and think while he has the privilege of changing his mind, if he is wrong, than it is to go on like a madman and be cast into the prison-house of hell. Then he will have to think; yes, memory will be keen then to act, but it will be too late to make any change.

I have been twice at the point of death. I was drowning once, and just as I was going down the third time I was rescued. In the twinkling of an eye my whole life came flashing across my mind. I cannot tell you how it was. I cannot tell you how a whole life can be crowded into a second of time; but everything I had done from my earliest childhood—it all came flashing across my mind. And I believe, that when God touches the secret spring of memory, every one of our sins will come back, and if they have not been blotted out by the blood of the Lord Jesus Christ, they will haunt us as eternal ages roll on. We talk about our forgetting, but we cannot forget if God says, "Remember!" We talk about the recording angel keeping the record of our life. I have an idea that when we get to heaven or into eternity, we will find that recording angel has been ourselves. God will make every one of us keep our own record. These memories will keep the record, and when God shall say, "Son, remember," it will all flash across our mind. It won't be God who will condemn us, it will be ourselves. We shall condemn ourselves, and we shall stand before God speechless.

There is a man in prison. He has been there five years. Ask that man what makes the prison so terrible to him. Ask him if it is the walls and the iron gates—ask him if it is his hard work, and he will tell you *no;* he will tell you what makes the prison so terrible to him is *memory*. And I have an idea that if we got down into the lost world, we would find that is what makes hell so terrible—the remembrance that they once heard the Gospel, that they once had Christ offered to them, that they once had the privilege of being saved, but they made light of the Gospel, they neglected salvation, they rejected the offer of mercy, and now if they would they could not.

A MISSIONARY SPIRIT IN HELL

We find this rich man had a desire to get out of that place of torment. He had a missionary spirit when he got there, for he said,

"Send some one to my father's house, and warn my five brethren. Oh, send some one to tell them not to come to this place of torment!"

Yes, it would have been better if he had had a missionary spirit before he had got there! It would be better for you that you should wake up and come to the Lord Jesus Christ, and go to work to save your friends while you are on praying ground, and in this world. Your missionary spirit won't help you when you are in hell; it won't help you when you are in the lost world. Yes, memory, memory! "Son, remember."

CAIN'S MEMORY

If Cain is in that lost world to-night, no doubt he can remember the pleading of his brother Abel. He can remember how he looked when he smote him—he can hear that piercing cry to-night; he has not forgotten it. All these long years Cain remembers what he might have been, how he despised the God of grace, and how he lost his soul. Thousands of years have rolled away, but still Cain has to think; he cannot help but think.

I have no doubt that Judas remembers how Christ preached that sermon he heard on the mountain, how Christ looked when He wept over Jerusalem, and he can see those tears to-night, he can hear that voice as He cried over Jerusalem, "O Jerusalem, Jerusalem, thou that killest the prophets, and stonest them which are sent unto thee, how often would I have gathered thy children together, even as a hen gathereth her chickens under her wings, and ye would not!" He hears that cry; he can see that kind, mild, gentle look of the Son of God. He can hear that voice as Christ said to him in Gethsemane,

"Betrayest thou the Master with a kiss?"

Yes, memory is at work. His memory woke up before he died, when he went out and destroyed himself, taking his remorse and despair with him into the lost world.

Noah's Contemporaries

Do you think those antediluvians have forgotten how Noah pleaded with them? They laughed at the ark. I have no doubt, if you had gone and preached to them a week before the flood, and told them that there was a hell, not one would have believed it. If you had told them that there was to be a deluge, and that God was going to sweep them away from the earth, they would not have believed it. But did it change the fact? Did not the flood come and take them all away?

You might have gone to Sodom and told the Sodomites that God was going to destroy Sodom, and they would have laughed at you, just as men make light of and laugh at hell. But did it change the fact? Did not God destroy the cities of the plain?

So with Jerusalem. Christ told how destruction would come upon it, and they mocked at Him and crucified Him. But look down the stream of time! In forty short years Titus came up against that city and besieged it, and there were a million that perished within it. Yes, those Jerusalem sinners can remember in the lost world to-night how Christ wept over Jerusalem, how He walked their streets, how He went into the temple and preached, and how He pleaded with them to escape for their life, and to flee the damnation of hell; but they mocked on, they laughed on, they made light until it was too late, and they are gone now.

Oh, may God wake up this audience, and may every man and woman here before it is too late escape for their lives! "How shall we escape," says the apostle, "if we neglect so great salvation?"

No Bible in the Lost World

There will be no Bible in the lost world to be a lamp to your feet and a light to your path, to guide you to eternal mansions. You make light of the Bible now; you laugh at its teachings; but bear in mind, there will be no Bible in the lost world. You have a Bible here. Had you not better take it now, had you not better read it, had you not better believe it?

I have not any doubt if a man had gone to that rich man a week before he was taken away he would have told you he did not believe in the Bible, he did not believe in a place of torment, he did not believe a word of it. But did that change the fact? He found it out when it was too late. And there was no Bible there to help him out.

There was no minister there to go and preach to him. Yes, bear in mind, if you get into that lost world, there will be no minister to pray for you, no earnest sermons preached there; it will be too late then.

There will be no Sabbath school teacher there. I am speaking now to some young people that are in the Sabbath school, and who have praying teachers. Bear in mind, you will have no teacher there to weep over you, to pray for you, to plead with you to come to Christ.

I may be speaking to some young man who has had some friend come and put his hand upon his shoulder, and ask him to come to Christ. You made light of that, young man. You laughed at him, and you cavilled at him. Bear in mind, there will be no friend to come and put his hand upon your shoulder, and speak loving words to you there. "Son, remember." If you have friends that are anxious for your soul's salvation here, and they are pleading for you, treat them kindly; you will not have them in that lost world. Do not laugh at them; it is God that sent the loving message to you.

I may be speaking to some young man who has a godly, praying mother. You are hasting to ruin, and breaking a mother's heart. Oh, young man, make that mother's heart glad to-night by telling her you have accepted her God as your God, her Saviour as your Saviour, that you are not going down to death and ruin, but that you will meet her in glory. Oh, may God meet every soul in this assembly, and may every eye and heart be opened to receive the truth!

You come here to-night to hear Mr. Sankey sing, "Jesus of Nazareth Passeth By"; but bear in mind, you will not hear that song in the lost world; or, if you do, it will not be true—He does not pass that way. To-night He is passing by! I beg of you, do not make light of the Lord Jesus and His offer of mercy. He comes to save you from a terrible hell. He wants to redeem every soul here to-night.

And now while I am speaking, hundreds and thousands of Christians are lifting their hearts silently to God for your salvation. May God answer their prayers, and may there be many to-night that shall be saved. Now you have a golden opportunity. Jesus is truly passing this way. Why do you doubt that He has been in our midst to-night? There has not been a night that a great many have not gone into the inquiry-room and have taken us by the hand, and said, "I have accepted Christ, I have found Him to-night," showing that the Lord Jesus Christ is in our midst. He is saving some; why should not He save you? And while He is passing, and so many are believing on Him, why won't you receive Him? My friends, God does not want you to perish, He wants you to be saved. God does not want a soul in this vast assembly to be lost, He wants every one to be in glory. And if you will accept His Son as a gift from Him, if you will accept the Lord Jesus, you can be saved.

An Unbelieving Mother

I was standing by the inquiry-room door in another place a few months ago, and I saw a lady weeping. I spoke to her; but a woman seized her by the hand and pushed her away from me. I said,

"What is the trouble?"

"Why," she said, "this is my daughter, and I don't want her to be associated with Christians; I hate Christians."

I tried to reason with that mother, but she pulled her daughter away weeping, the daughter pleading with the mother to stay.

Is there such a mother here to-night? May God have mercy upon you! It is a thousand times better for your daughters and your children to be associated with Christians than it is to have them go down to death and be associated with fiends as eternal ages go on. All workers of iniquity shall be cast into the lake of fire, but those whose names are written in the book of life shall have a right to the tree of life, and shall walk the crystal pavement of heaven. Oh, may God help you to be wise to-night, to flee from your old companions and associates, and lay hold of eternal life! Do not trifle with this great subject. Be wise, and accept salvation as it comes from God.

AN UNFILIAL SON

I was once told of a father that had a son who had broken his mother's heart. After her death he went on from bad to worse. One night he was going out to spend it in vice, and the old man went to the door as the younger one was going out, and said,

"My son, I want to ask a favor of you to-night. You have not spent one night with me since your mother was buried, and I have been so lonesome without her and without you, and now I want to have you spend tonight with me. I want to have a talk with you about the future."

The young man said, "No, father, I do not want to stay; it is gloomy here at home."

"Won't you stay for my sake?"

The son said he would not.

At last the old man said, "If I cannot persuade you to stay, if you are determined to go down to ruin, and to break my heart as you have your mother's—for these gray hairs cannot stand it much longer—you shall not go without my making one more effort to save you."

He threw open the door, and laid himself upon the threshold, and said,

"If you go out to-night you must go over this old body of mine."

What did that young man do? Why, he leaped over the father, and on to ruin he went.

Now there is not a man or woman here who would not say that young man was an ungrateful wretch. Did you ever think that God has given His Son? Yes, He has laid Him (as it were) right across your path that you might not go down to hell; and if there is a soul in this assembly that goes to hell, you must go over the murdered body of God's Son, you must trample the blood of Christ under your feet. No sooner did the news reach heaven that Adam had fallen, than God came down and made a way of escape. God so loved the world that He gave Christ to die that you and I might live. Do not make light of that blessed Saviour. Do not sit here and have that scornful look upon your brow, but lift up your heart to God, and say, "God be merciful to me a sinner." Receive the gift of God!

If the Spirit of God is striving with you, let me plead with you. Treat Him kindly. Bear in mind that God has said that His Spirit shall not always strive. There have been many, I believe, that have been awakened, and the Spirit of God has been striving with you; and now let me plead with you as a friend— just give yourself up to the leading of the Spirit of God. The Spirit of God will lead us aright; He never makes any mistake. God has sent Him from heaven into this world to lead us out of darkness into light, and the Spirit is drawing you to Christ. Do not resist Him; do not reject Him. I do not ask you to think or to believe what I say; all I ask is, believe what God tells you; believe what the Spirit of God will reveal to you about Christ; and if the Spirit of God is striving with you, do not quench or resist Him, but to-night just open the door of your heart and let Him come in, and it will be a thousand times better for you in this life and in the life to come.

A few years ago I was about to close a meeting, and said,

"Are there any here that would like to have me remember them in prayer? I would like to have them arise!"

A man rose and when I saw him stand up, my heart leaped in me for joy. I had been anxious for him a long time. I went to him as soon as the meeting was over, and took him by the hand, and said,

"You are coming out for God, are you not?"

"I want to," he said, "and I have made up my mind to be a Christian, only there is one thing stands in my way."

"What is that?" I said.

"Well," he said, "I lack moral courage. If he had been here to-night (naming a friend of his), I should not have risen; and I am afraid when he hears I have risen for prayer he will begin to laugh at me, and I won't have the moral courage to stand up for Christ."

I said, "If Christ is what He is represented in the Bible, He is worth standing up for; and if heaven is what we are told it is in the Bible, it is worth our living for." He said he lacked moral courage, and was trembling from head to foot. I thought he was just at the very threshold of heaven, and that one step more was going to take him in, and that he would take the step that night. I talked and prayed with him, and the Spirit seemed to be striving mightily with him, but he did not get light. Night after night he came, and the Spirit still strove with him; but just that one thing kept him—he lacked moral courage. At last the Spirit of God who had striven with him so mightily seemed to leave him, and there was no more striving. He left off coming to church, was off among his old companions, and would not meet me in the street—he was ashamed to do so.

About six months afterwards I got a message from him, and found him on what he thought his dying-bed. He wanted to know if there was any hope for him at the eleventh hour. I tried to tell him there was hope for any man that would accept Christ. I prayed with him, and day after day visited him.

Contrary to all expectations, he began to recover. When he was convalescent, finding him one day sitting in front of his house, I sat by his side, and said,

"You will soon be well enough to come up to the church, and when you are, you will come up, and you are just going to confess Christ boldly, are you not?"

"Well," said he, "I promised God when I was on what we thought my dying-bed I would serve Him, and I made up my mind to be a Christian; but I am not going to be one just now. Next spring I am going over by Lake Michigan, and I am going to buy a farm, and settle down, and then I am going to be a Christian." "How dare you talk in that way!" I said. "How do you know you are going to live till next spring? Have you a lease of your life?" "I never was better than I am now," he said, "I am a little weak, but I will soon have my strength. I have a fresh lease of my life, and will be well for a good many years yet."

"It seems to me you are tempting God," and I pleaded with him to come out boldly.

"No," he said, "the fact is, I have not the courage to face my old companions, and I cannot serve God in Chicago." "If God has not grace enough to keep you in Chicago," I said, "He has not in Michigan."

I urged him then and there to surrender soul and body to the Lord Jesus, but the more I urged him the more irritated he got, till at last he said,

"Well, you need not trouble yourself any more about my soul; I will attend to that. If I am lost, it will be my own fault. I will take the risk."

A Fearful Death-Bed

I left him, and within a week I got a message from his wife. Going to the house, I met her at the door weeping. I said,

"What is the trouble?"

"Oh, sir, I have just had a council of physicians here, and they have all given my husband up to die; they say he cannot live."

"Does he want to see me?" I asked.

"No."

"Why did you send for me?"

"Oh," she said, "I cannot bear to see him die in this terrible state of mind."

"What is his state of mind?"

"He says that his damnation is sealed, and he will be in hell in a little while."

I went into the room, but he turned his head away.

"How is it with you?" I said.

Not a word! He was as silent as death. I spoke the second time, but he made no response. I looked him in the face, and called him by name, and said,

"Will you not tell me how it is with you?"

He turned, fixed that awful deathly look upon me, and, pointing to the stove, he said,

"My heart is as hard as the iron in that stove. It is too late! My damnation is sealed, and I shall be in hell in a little while."

"Don't talk so," I said, "you can be saved now if you will."

"Don't you mock me, I know better," he replied.

I talked with him, and quoted promise after promise, but he said not one was for him.

"Christ has come knocking at the door of my heart many a time, and the last time He came I promised to let Him in, and when I got well I turned away from Him again, and now I have to perish without Him."

I talked, but saw that I was doing no good, and so I threw myself on my knees.

"You can pray for my wife and my children," he said, "you need not pray for me. It is a waste of your time. It is too late!"

I tried to pray, but it seemed as if what he said was true—as if the heavens were as brass over me.

I rose and took his hand. It seemed to me as if I were bidding farewell to a friend that I never was to see again in time or in eternity.

He lingered till the sun went down. His wife told me his end was terrible. All that he was heard to say were these fearful words, "The harvest is past, the summer is ended, and I am not saved!" Just as the sun was sinking behind those western prairies he was going into the arms of death. As he was expiring, his wife noticed that his lips were quivering, he was trying to say something. She reached over her ear, and all she could hear was, "The harvest is past, the summer is ended, and I am not saved!" and the angels bore him to the judgment.

He lived a Christless life, he died a Christless death. We wrapped him in a Christless shroud and nailed him in a Christless coffin, and bore him to a Christless grave. Oh, how dark! Oh, how sad!

I may be speaking to some one to-night, and the harvest may be passing with you, the summer may be ending—oh, be wise to-night and accept the Lord Jesus Christ as your Saviour! Believe that He bore your sins in His own body on the cross, and be saved. May God's blessing rest upon us all, and may we meet in glory, is the prayer of my heart!

"COME"

Preface

THIS IS ONE of those sermons by Mr. Moody in which a series of texts are used, all related to a single theme, and sometimes all using a single word. He often preached on "The 'I Wills' of Christ"; "The Six 'One Things' "; "The Beholds." One-eighth of this sermon is devoted to the interview with the infidel and, which is not true with many of Mr. Moody's sermons, it closes with a poem. There are, I believe, nine illustrations used in this sermon. Inasmuch as most of the texts which he used are not identified, perhaps the reader will be glad for a list of them in the order of their occurrence: Isaiah 55:3; Revelation 3:20; John 1:39; Isaiah 1:18; Matthew 11:28; John 7:37; John 21:12; Matthew 22:4; Matthew 25:34; Genesis 6:18; Revelation 22:17. The text I have used here is found in *Great Joy*, pp. 479-92. It is also found in *Moody's Great Sermons* (1899), pp. 264-75; *Sermons, Addresses, and Prayers* (1877), pp. 504-11; with the title "A Chime of Gospel Bells" in *Sovereign Grace*, pp. 74-94; and *Gospel Awakening* (1879), pp. 536-45.

"Come"

WE HAVE FOR OUR SUBJECT this afternoon the precious little word "Come." I want to call your attention first to the "Come" in the 53rd chapter of the prophecies of Isaiah.* "Incline your ear, and come unto me: hear, and your soul shall live; and I will make an everlasting covenant with you, even the sure mercies of David."

"Incline your ear, and come unto me; hear, and your soul shall live." Now, I find if we get people to listen—to pause and hear the voice of God, it isn't long before they are willing to follow that voice; but it is so hard to get people to stop and listen for a moment. The din of the world makes such a noise that the people don't hear the voice—that still small voice. He says, "Incline your ear, and come unto me." Now, if we could only get all the friends in this audience to incline their ears this afternoon—not only your natural ears but the ears of your soul, you could be saved to-day. But Satan does not want you to do this; he does all he can to keep your ears from hearing. He makes you think about yourself, about your sons, your homes; but, my friends, let us forget all those things to-day—let us forget all our surroundings, and close our eyes to the world, and just try and listen to the word of God, and come and hear what He has to say. "Incline your ear, and come unto me: hear and your soul shall live." Now, let us turn to the tenth chapter of Romans, where we see, "Faith cometh by hearing, and hearing by the word of God." Now, it is not my words I want to have you to listen to—it is not my words I want you to hear this afternoon, but I want you to hear the words of this loving King who calls you to Himself. What does He say? In another place he says: "Behold, I stand at the door, and knock; if any man hear my voice, and open the door, I will come in to him, and sup with him, and he with me," or "if any woman," or any one; that's what it means, my friends—"hear my voice, and open the door,

*Editor's note: This is the only sermon that I have read in the many volumes of Mr. Moody's published sermons in which the text is incorrectly given. The reference here is to Isaiah 53:3 but it actually is 55:3. This must have been a mistake of the reporter, for Mr. Moody knew the 53rd chapter of Isaiah by heart, and he certainly knew this text was not a part of that chapter.

I will come in to her, and will sup with her and she with me."
I heard of a little child some time ago who was burned. The
mother had gone out and left her three children at home. The
eldest left the room, and the remaining two began to play with
the fire, and set the place in a blaze. When the youngest of the
two saw what she had done she went into a little cupboard and
fastened herself in. The remaining child went to the door and
knocked and knocked, crying to her to open the door and let her
take her out of the burning building, but she was too frightened
to do it. It seems to me as if this was the way with hundreds and
thousands in this city. He stands and knocks, but they've got
their hearts barred and bolted, because they don't know that He
has come only to bless them. May God help you to hear, and if
you listen to Him and bring your burdens to Him, He will bless
you. He is able to open the ears of every one here if you let Him
in. I was up here at the hotel the other night, and I had the door
locked and bolted, and some one came and rapped. I shouted
"Come in!" The man tried to come in, but he couldn't; I had
to get up and unlock the door before he could enter. That's the
way with many people to-day. They've got the door bolted and
barred; but if you only open it to Him, He will come in.

"If any man hear my voice, and open the door, I will come in
and sup with him and he with me." Now, my friends, can you
hear it? Can you hear God's voice speaking through His own
Word? "Incline your ear and come unto me." Just listen. You
know sometimes, when you hear a man speaking whose voice you
don't hear very well, and you want to hear every word the man
says, you put your hand up to your ear to catch the sound clearer.
Now, listen. God says, "Incline your ear, and come unto me:
hear, and your soul shall live; and I will make an everlasting
covenant with you." Now, is it not true? Can't you hear that
loving voice speaking to you, and won't you obey that voice and
let Him save you? But I can imagine some of you saying, "I
can't hear anything." Take your ears to Him and He will make
you hear.

Now let me take you to another course. While John and his
disciples were standing, Jesus came along, and John said: "Behold the Lamb of God!" and Jesus said: "What seek ye?" "Where

dwellest thou?" he asked; to which He replied; "Come and see"; and they just obeyed Him and never left Him. My friends, if I could introduce you to Christ—could just get you to catch one glimpse of Him; if you could but see the King in all His beauty; if you could but see Him in all His loveliness, you would never forsake Him, for we "shall grow up before him as a tender plant, and as a root out of a dry ground: he hath no form nor comeliness; and when we shall see him, there is no beauty that we should desire him." Follow Him as your Saviour. In order to appreciate Him you have to be brought to Him, but if sin has come between you and Him, I cannot tell you anything about Him. It is just like telling a blind man about the beauties of nature, the loveliness of the flowers, or of the world. That is the way, if sin stands between you and Him, and when Christians try to tell you about the beauties of Christianity they fail, but if you come and have an interview with Him you will see that you cannot help but love Him; you will see that you cannot but forsake all and follow Him. I remember once hearing of a child who was born blind. He grew up to be almost a man, when a skillful physician thought he could give the man his sight. He was put under the doctor's treatment, and for a long time he worked, till at last he succeeded. But he wouldn't let the man see the light of the sun all at once, lest it would strike him blind. It had to be done gradually. So he put a lot of bandages upon his eyes and removed one after another until the last one was reached, and when it was taken off the young man began to see. When he saw the beauties of the world he upbraided his friends for not telling him of the beauties of nature. "Why, we tried to tell you about the beauties of the world, but we could not," they said. And so it is with us. All that we can do is to tell you to come and see—come and see the loveliness of Christ.

I can imagine some of you saying, "I am blind, I cannot see any beauty in Him." Bring your blindness to Him as you bring your deafness and He will give you sight, as He did with the blind Bartimeus—as He did with all the blind men on earth. There was never a blind man who came to Him requesting his sight whose request was not granted, and there is not a blind soul in this assembly but will be healed if you come to Him. He says that's what He came for, to give sight to the blind. If you cannot see any beauty in Him pray to God to give you sight.

The next "Come" is in the prophecies of Isaiah. "Come now, and let us reason together, saith the Lord: though your sins be as scarlet, they shall be as white as snow; though they be red like crimson, they shall be as wool." I find a great many people say their reason stands between them and God. Now, let me say here, the religion of Jesus is a matter of revelation, not of investigation. No one ever found out Christ by reason. It is a matter of revelation. Now see what He says, "Come now"—that means this afternoon—"though your sins be as scarlet, they shall be as white as snow." Now He puts a pardon in the sinner's face. "Your sins may be as scarlet, they shall be white as snow." Take the scarlet in that lady's shawl. It is a fast color. You cannot wash it out and make it white; if you tried you would only destroy the shawl. But He will make your sins white as snow, though they be as scarlet, if you come to Him. Just come to Him as you are, and instead of reasoning, ask Him to take them away. Then He will reason it out with you. The natural man does not understand spiritual things, but when a man is born of the Spirit, then it is that the spiritual things are brought out to him. A great many people want to investigate—want to reason out the Bible from back to back, but He wants us first to take a pardon. That's God's method of reasoning. He puts a pardon in the face of the sinner. "Come now." Do you think there is not reason in this? Suppose the whole plan of salvation was reasoned out to you, why death might step in before the end of the reasoning was reached. So God puts a pardon first. If you will be influenced to-day you will just bring your reason to Him, and ask Him to give you wisdom to see divine things, and He will do it. "If any of you lack wisdom, let him ask of God, that giveth to all men liberally, and upbraideth not; and it shall be given liberally." The idea, that this reason that God hath given man should keep him from Christ.

A number of years ago as I was coming out of a daily prayer meeting in one of our Western cities, a lady came up to me and said, "I want to have you see my husband and ask him to come to Christ." She said, "I want to have you go and see him." She told me his name, and it was of a man I had heard of before. "Why," said I, "I can't go and see your husband. He is a booked infidel. I can't argue with him. He is a good deal older than I am, and it would be out of place. Then I am not much for infidel argument." "Well, Mr. Moody," she says, "that ain't what he wants. He's got enough of that. Just ask him to come to the Saviour." She urged me so hard and so strong, that I consented to go. I went to the office where the Judge was doing business, and told him what I had come for. He laughed at me. "You are very foolish," he said, and began to argue with me. I said, "I don't think it will be profitable for me to hold an argument with you. I have just one favor I want to ask of you, and that is, that when you are converted you will let me know." "Yes," said he, "I will do that. When I am converted, I will let you know"—with a good deal of sarcasm.

I went off, and requests for prayer were sent here and to Fulton Street, New York, and I thought the prayer there and of that wife would be answered if mine were not. A year and a half after I was in that city, and a servant came to the door and said: "There is a man in the front parlor who wishes to see you." I found the Judge there. He said: "I promised I would let you know when I was converted. I've been converted." "Well," said I, "I'm glad to hear it! Tell me all about it." I had heard it from other lips, but I wanted to hear it from his own. He said his wife had gone out to a meeting one night and he was home alone, and while he was sitting there by the fire he thought, "Supposing my wife is right, and my children are right: suppose there is a heaven and hell, and I shall be separated from them." His first thought was: "I don't believe a word of it." The second thought came, "You believe in the God that created you, and that the God that created you is able to teach you. You believe that God can give you life." "Yes, the God that created me can give me life. I was too proud to get down on my knees by the fire, and I said, 'O God, teach me.' And as I prayed, I don't understand it, but it began to get very dark, and my heart got very heavy. I was afraid to tell my wife when she came to bed and I pretended to be asleep. She kneeled down beside that bed and I knew she was praying for me. I kept crying, 'O God, save me; O God, take away this burden,' but it grew darker, and the load grew heavier and heavier. All the way to my office I kept crying, 'O God, take away this load of guilt.' I gave my clerks a holiday, and just closed my office and locked the door. I fell down on my face: I cried in agony to the Lord, 'O Lord, for Christ's sake, take away this guilt.' I don't know how it was, but it began to grow very light. I said, I wonder if this isn't what they call conversion. I think I will go and ask the minister if I am not converted. I met my wife at the door and said, 'My dear, I've been converted.' She looked in amazement. 'Oh it's a fact, I've been converted!' We went into that drawing-room and knelt down by the sofa and prayed to God to bless us." The old Judge said to me, the tears trickling down his cheeks, "Mr. Moody, I've enjoyed life more in the last three months than in all the years of my life put together." If there is an infidel here—if there is a skeptical one here, ask God to give wisdom to come now. Let us reason together, and if you become acquainted with God the day will not go before you receive light from Him.

The next "Come" I want to call your attention to is a very sweet one. He says, "Come and reason," "Come and see," and now we have "Come and rest." What this world wants is rest. Every man, every woman is in pursuit of it, and how many of us have found? How many are bearing burdens about our hearts always—how many have come into this hall to-day with a great burden on their hearts? What does He say: "Come unto me, all ye that labour and are heavy laden, and I will give you rest." Now a great many people have an idea that they get rid of their burdens themselves, but they must come to Him if they want to be relieved. That's what Christ came for. Come to Him. "He hath borne our griefs and carried our sorrows." There could not be a sweeter "Come" than this. How many mothers are bearing burdens for their children—how many because of their sons, or perhaps you have husbands who have proved unfaithful, or may be you are widows who have been without support. The future may look dark to you: but hear the loving voice of the Saviour, "Come unto me, all ye that labour and are heavy laden, and I will give you rest." There is not a soul here—I don't care

what the burden may be—in this vast audience, but can lay their
burden on the Lord Jesus Christ, and He will bear it for you.
We can be released; we have found a resting place, and that is in
the loving bosom of the Lord Jesus Christ. There is a hymn
written by Dr. Andrew Bonar which can express this much better
than I can. Let me read it:

> I heard the voice of Jesus say:
>   "Come unto me and rest;
> Lay down, thou weary one, lay down
>   Thy head upon my breast."
>
> I came to Jesus as I was,
>   Weary and worn and sad;
> I found in Him a resting-place,
>   And He has made me glad.
>
> I heard the voice of Jesus say:
>   "Behold I freely give
> The living water—thirsty one,
>   Stoop down and drink and live!"
>
> I came to Jesus and I drank
>   Of that life-giving stream;
> My thirst was quenched, my soul revived
>   And now I live in Him.
>
> I heard the voice of Jesus say:
>   "I am this dark world's light;
> Look unto Me, thy morn shall rise,
>   And all thy day be bright."
>
> I looked at Jesus and I found
>   In Him my Star, my Sun.
> And in that light of Life I'll walk
>   Till travelling days are done.

Oh, my friends, if you want rest to-day, come to Him. He
stands with His arms outstretched and says: "Come to me and
rest." Does the world satisfy you? Are not the griefs of this
world crushing many a heart here? Hear the voice of Jesus:
"Come and rest." The world cannot take it from you; the world's

crosses and trials will not tear it from you; He will give you peace and comfort and rest if you but come.

The next "Come" is "come and drink and eat." You don't have to pay anything. You know it is hard for a man to get a tax on water unless when it has to be brought into the city. But this water is always without price, and salvation is like a river, flowing at the feet of every one; and all you have to do is to stoop down and drink of this living water and never die. The world cannot give you comfort—cannot give you water to satisfy your thirst, and every man and woman in this world is thirsty. That's the way our places of amusement are filled. People are constantly thirsting for something. But how are they filled with those amusements? They are as thirsty as ever. But if they drink the waters that He offers they will have a fountain in them springing up into everlasting life. I remember coming down a river with some wounded soldiers. The water was very muddy, and as we had no filters they had to drink the dirty water, which did not satisfy their thirst. I remember a soldier saying, "O that I had a draught of water from my father's well." If you drink of the living water your soul will never thirst again. Not only does He say, "Come and drink of that living water," but He says, "Come and eat." In the fifty-fifth chapter of Isaiah you are invited to come and eat. You know all that the children of Israel had to do in the wilderness was just to pick up the manna and eat. They didn't have to make it. And people had just to stoop down and pick up the manna and eat, and drink from the flinty rock when the water flowed. And to-day the provision is brought to the door of your hearts. You haven't to go down to the earth for it, or to go up to the skies for it. It is here, and all you've got to do is to eat.

You know almost the last words of Christ after His resurrection, when, having a little fish, He said to His disciples, "Come and dine." Oh, what a sweet invitation—the invitation of the Master to His disciples, "Come and dine." I invite you now to come and dine with Him; He will quench that thirst; He will satisfy your hunger, and all you've got to do is to take Him at His word.

Is there a poor thirsty one here to-day? I bid you come and

drink of the fountain of living water; I bid you come and eat of the heavenly bread; yes, the bread made in heaven, the bread that angels feed on—Christ Himself is the bread of life.

Now, many people make a great mistake about accepting Christ. They think they've got something to do; think they've got to do some work, or that they've got to pray and wrestle before taking Him; they think it is a question of performances whether they are saved or not. Now, it is a question of simply taking what God offers you. I remember when I was out on the Pacific coast, a man took me through his house, out on his lands, and showed me his orchards, and then said: "Mr. Moody, you are a guest of mine, and I want you to feel perfectly at home, do what you like." Well, after this man said this, you don't suppose if I wanted an orange I was going under the tree to pray that it would fall into my pocket? I just went up boldly and plucked what I wanted. And so the bread of heaven is offered to us, and all we've got to do is to go boldly up and take it. This is what God wants you to do. Everything is prepared for you.

There is a class, too, who say: "But I'm afraid I'll not hold out." How many people are stumbling over this! Now, if you come boldly up to the throne you'll get all the support you need—"Let us therefore come boldly unto the throne of grace, that we may obtain mercy, and find grace to help in time of need." There is a passage for you; that ought to be sufficient. And there is not a woman here to-day but can be kept, from this very day and this very hour, from evil—"For I the Lord thy God will keep you, without spot or wrinkle, and without blemish." Some of the vilest men who have ever trodden this earth have been saved with the grace of God. Some have been kept sixty or seventy years merely by the grace of God, and never wavered. "Come boldly to the throne of grace" and you will get power. That is sufficient. Won't you take Him at His word? It seems to me that it is madness not to take the gift offered us by God.

Let me call attention to another "Come." My friends, the Bible is full of them, and you can't say if you don't come there have been no invitations. He says: "Come to the marriage." Now, you young ladies like marriages pretty well. Let a marriage come off in a church, and hundreds will be there; and probably

next night, at the prayer meeting, there will scarcely be a dozen
of you present. Now here is a marriage, and there is not a lady
here whom God does not want to be present at the marriage
feast. There is an invitation. And here is another "Come":
"Come and inherit the kingdom prepared for you from the foundation of the world." God has got an inheritance for every one
of you. The time will soon come, if you accept Christ and become as His bride, when you shall hear the voice of Him saying
to you: "Come and inherit the kingdom prepared for you from
the foundation of the world." What a mistake it will be, my
friends, if you will not hear that invitation given to you! There
is an inheritance incorruptible in the heavens, a building not
made with hands, and He wants every one to enter into this inheritance, and so it is your privilege to be present at the marriage feast and receive the inheritance if you will.

You know the first "Come" in the Bible is in regard to salvation. It was given to Noah; God said, "Come thou, and all thy
house into the ark," not a part of them, but "all thy house."
That is the first "Come" in the Bible, and all through that
blessed book it is repeated; and now we come to the last one.
It seems as if the Bible was created by this word "come." "The
Spirit and the bride say, Come. And let him that is athirst
come. And whosoever will, let him taste the water of life freely."
There is our invitation, as broad as the world itself. And if God
says you are to come in there, no power in heaven, or earth, or
hell can stop you! He bids you come. Now bear in mind it is
your sins God wants, and not your faith. You have nothing
about you that He wants except your sins. People are continually
trying to come to Him by their faith, by their feelings, by their
tears, by their good deeds, by their works; but you have to come
to Him just as you are. There is not a woman present but can
roll off every sin and leave them in this tabernacle.

Now the question comes, What right have you to come? Why,
because the King invites you. Suppose Queen Victoria had sent
me an invitation to be present at Windsor at a feast given in
honor of the marriage of one of her sons to a princess of Russia.
I take the cars to New York, then the boat to Liverpool, then I
would run down to London, where I would get the train to

Windsor Castle. There is a sentry walking up and down in front of the gate. If I hadn't my invitation he would refuse me admittance; but there is not a soldier in the British army can keep me out, because I've got the Queen's invitation. But suppose the man looks at me and says: "You can't go into the presence of the Queen with those clothes; you are not fit to stand before the Queen." That is none of his business; that's hers. So the invitation comes from Him, and He wants you to come and He will clothe you in garments fit for His presence. You will be stripped of every rag of self-righteousness, and a robe of spotlessness will be put upon you.

A great many people say, "I want to become clean before I come to Christ." Now, my friends, that is the devil's work. He tries to get people to believe that they can't come without getting rid of their sins, but as I've said, all through the Scriptures He bids you come as you are. We cannot take away our sins; come to Him and He will blot them out. A few years ago in London, there used to be a good many little children stolen to act as chimney sweeps. A child was stolen from a wealthy family, and a great reward was offered, but he couldn't be found. This child had been kidnapped. One day he was sent up a chimney and came down on the other side, and into a beautiful room. The little fellow was bewildered. A lady was sitting there, and recognized him as her son, and although the little fellow was covered with smut, she ran to him, and drew him to her bosom, and that is the way Christ will receive you. You needn't try to get rid of one particle of sin. He wants to save you as you are. "Whosoever will, let him come and drink of the waters of life freely." Will you come to-day? The Spirit and the bride invite you this afternoon. Now I want to ask you what are you going to do with these ten loving invitations to-day—"Come and hear," "Come and see," "Come and reason," "Come and rest," "Come and eat and drink," "Come and dine," "Come and find grace," "Come unto the marriage," "Come and inherit the kingdom prepared for you from the foundation of the world," "Whosoever will, let him come." Ask God to help you to come to-day. If I were in your place I would settle this question before I left this building; I would just press up to the kingdom of God and take

Him at His word. Now would you just all lift up your hearts in prayer. Let every Christian pray for every soul here to-day out of Christ. Let us now just unite in this one petition that every soul in this building may come to Christ to-day.

DANIEL

Preface

THIS IS THE ONLY SERMON in this volume from which some paragraphs have been removed. I have taken this material from the well-known volume, *Bible Characters,* in which six chapters are devoted to Daniel, of which I have used material from two successive chapters. I thought this was better than taking a single brief message on Daniel. There is no question that of all the characters of the Old and New Testaments, Mr. Moody loved to preach most often on Daniel. Those who have reported hearing these sermons all witness to the fact that his descriptions were so gripping that the audiences seemed utterly hushed and then deeply moved as the experiences of this prophet were unfolded, especially his being cast into the den of lions. My own opinion is that probably Mr. Moody's most graphic sentences are to be found in these sermons on Daniel. It is very significant that while he often preached from different chapters in Daniel, none of his printed sermons indicate that he ever preached from its great prophecies, especially those in chapters 2, 7 and 9. How greatly this material varied from time to time can be seen in the fact that a separate volume, *Daniel the Prophet,* issued in 1875, consisted of some-thirty-two pages, while the same volume issued in 1884 embraced sixty pages.

For other sermons on Daniel, see *Gospel Awakening* (1876), pp. 576-88; *Great Joy* (1879), pp. 134-56; *Great Redemption* (1889), pp. 215-33 (on the word "tekel"); *The Old Gospel and Other Addresses* (1882), pp. 133-51; *Sermons, Addresses, and Prayers* (1877), pp. 181-88; and E. L. Pell, *Dwight L. Moody* (1900), pp. 589-600. There are sermons on Daniel's prayer in *To All People* (1877), pp. 88-94, and on the soul-winner in *The Overcoming Life and Other Sermons* (1896), pp. 53-66. There are two sermons on Daniel in addition to one on "tekel" in *Bible Readings Delivered in San Francisco and Oakland* by D. L. Moody et al. (1881), pp. 120-28 ,150-56.

Daniel

WE FIND THAT DARIUS—who was probably one of the high military commanders engaged in the siege of Babylon—takes the kingdom, while Cyrus is off conquering other parts of the world. As soon as he attains the throne he makes his arrangements for governing the country. He divides the kingdom into one hundred and twenty provinces; and he appoints a prince or ruler over each province; and over the princes he puts three presidents to see that these rulers do no damage to the king, and do not swindle the government. And over these three he places Daniel, as president of the presidents. Very possibly Darius knew the man. He may have been in former days at the court of Nebuchadnezzar; and if so, he probably considered Daniel an able and conscientious statesman. Anyhow, the king either knew, or was told, sufficient to justify his confidence. And now Daniel is again in office. He held in that day the highest position, under the sovereign, that any one could hold. He was next to the throne. If you will allow me the expression, he was the Bismarck or the Gladstone of the empire. He was Prime Minister; he was Secretary of State; and all important matters would pass through his hands.

We do not know how long he held that position. But sooner or later the other presidents and the princes grew jealous, and wanted Daniel out of the way. It was as if they had said, "Let us see if we cannot get this sanctimonious Hebrew removed: he has 'bossed' us along enough." You see he was so impracticable: they could do nothing with him. There were plenty of collectors and treasurers; but he kept such a close eye on them that they only made their salaries. There was no chance of plundering the government while he was at the head. He was president, and probably all the revenue accounts passed before him. No doubt these enemies wanted to form a "ring." And they may have talked somewhat after this fashion: "If it were not for this man we could form a 'ring'; and then, in three or four years, we could make enough to enable us to retire from office, and have a villa on the banks of the Euphrates; or we could go down to Egypt, and see something of the world. We could have plenty of money—all we should ever want, or our children either—if we could only just get control of the government, and manage things as we should like to. As things go now we only just get our exact dues; and it will take years and years for them to mount up to anything respectable. If we had matters in our own hands it would be different; for King Darius does not know half as much about the affairs of this empire as does this old Hebrew: and he watches our accounts so closely that we can get no advantage over the government. Down with this pious Jew!"

Probably these plotters met at night, for it generally happens that if men want to do any downright mean business they meet at night: darkness suits them best. The chief-president himself was not there: he had not been invited to meet them. Very likely some lawyer, who understood all about the laws of the Medes and Persians, stood up, and talked something after this fashion: "Gentlemen, I have got, I think, a plan that will work well, by which we may get rid of this old Hebrew. You know he will not serve any but the God of Abraham and Isaac."

And these plotters said one to another, "Now, let us get Darius to sign a decree that if any man make a request of any God or man—except of the King Darius—for thirty days, he shall be put into the lions' den. And let us all keep perfectly still about this matter, so that it won't get out. We must not tell our wives, for fear the news may get about the city: Daniel would find it all out; and he has more influence with the king than all the rest of us put together. The king would never sign the decree if he found out what the object was." Then they may have said, "We must draw it so tight that Darius will not be able to get out of it after he has once signed. We must make it so binding that if the king once signs we shall have that Daniel in the lions' den: and we will take good care that the lions shall be hungry."

When the mine is all ready, the conspirators come to the king, and open their business with flattering speech: "King Darius, live for ever!" When people approach me with smooth and oily words, I know they have something else coming—I know they have some purpose in telling me I am a good man. These plotters, perhaps, go on to tell the king how prosperous the realm is, and how much the people think of him.

They most likely tickled his vanity, and told him that he was the most popular man that had ever reigned in Babylon; and then they may have gone on to tell him how attached they were to him and his rule, and that they had been consulting together on what they could do to increase his popularity and make him more beloved; and now they had hit upon a plan that was almost sure to do it. They would point out that if no one called upon any god for thirty days, but only on him, the king, making him a god, it would render him the most popular monarch that had ever reigned in Babylonia; and his name would be handed down to posterity. And if he could get men to call upon his name for thirty days they would probably keep it up, and so permanently reckon him among the gods.

And now they are ready to let the news go forth; and it is not long before it spreads through the highways of Babylon. The men of the city knew the man: knew that he would not vacillate. They knew that the old man with the grey locks would not turn to the right hand or the left: they knew that if his enemies caught him in that way, he would not deny his God or turn away from Him: they knew that he was going to be true to his God.

Daniel was none of your sickly Christians of the nineteenth century: he was none of your weak-backed, none of your weak-kneed Christians: he had moral stamina and courage. I can imagine that aged white-haired Secretary of State sitting at his table going over the accounts of some of these rulers of provinces. Some of the timid, frightened Hebrews come to him, and say:

"Oh, Daniel, have you heard the latest news?"

"No. What is it?"

"What! Have you not been to the king's palace this morning?"

"No! I have not been to the palace to-day. What is the matter?"

"Well, there is a conspiracy against you. A lot of those princes have induced King Darius to sign a decree that if any man shall call upon any God in his kingdom within thirty days he shall be thrown to the lions. Their object is to have you cast into the den. Now if you can only get out of the way for a little time—if you will just quit Babylon for thirty days—it will advance both your own and the public interest. You are the chief secretary and treasurer—in fact, you are the principal member of the government: you are an important man, and can do as you please. Well now, just you get out of Babylon. Or, if you will stay in Babylon, do not let any one catch you on your knees. In any case do not pray at the window which looks towards Jerusalem; as you have been doing for the last fifty years. And if you will pray, close that window, draw a curtain over it; shut the door, and stop up every crevice. People are sure to be about your house listening."

How many men there are who are ashamed to be caught upon their knees! Many a man, if found upon his knees by the wife of his bosom, would jump right up and walk around the room as if he had no particular object in view. How many young men there are who come up from the country and enter upon city life, and have not the moral courage to go down on their knees before their roommates! How many young men say, "Don't ask me to get down on my knees at this prayer-meeting." Men have not the moral courage to be seen praying. They lack moral courage. Ah! thousands of men have been lost for lack of moral courage; have been lost because at some critical moment they shrank from going on their knees, and being seen and known as being worshipers of God—as being on the Lord's side. Ah, the fact is—we are a pack of cowards: that is what we are. Shame on the Christianity of the nineteenth century! It is a weak and sickly thing. Would to God that we had a host of men like Daniel living to-day!

Do you think that Daniel, after having walked with God for half a century or more, is going to turn round like that? Ten thousand times, No!

True as steel, that old man goes to his room three times a day. Mark you, he had time to pray. There is many a business man to-day who will tell you he has no time to pray: his business is so pressing that he cannot call his family around him, and ask God to bless them. He is so busy that he cannot ask God to keep him and them from the temptations of the present life—the temptations of every day. "Business is so pressing." I am reminded of the words of an old Methodist minister: "If you have so much business to attend to that you have no time to pray, depend upon it you have more business on hand than God ever intended you should have." But look at this man. He had the whole, or nearly the whole, of the king's business to attend to. He was Prime Minister, Secretary of State, and Secretary of the Treasury, all in one. He had to attend to all his own work; and to give an eye to the work of lots of other men. And yet he found time to pray: not just now and then, not once in a while, not just when he happened to have a few moments to spare, mark you—but "three times a day." Yes, he could take up the words of the fifty-fifth Psalm, and say:

> As for me, I will call upon God;
> And the Lord shall save me.
> Evening, and morning, and at noon, will I pray, and cry aloud:
> And he shall hear my voice.

Busy as he was, he found time to pray. And a man whose habit it is to call upon God saves time, instead of losing it. He has a clearer head, a more collected mind, and can act with more decision when circumstances require it.

So Daniel went to his room three times a day: he trod that path so often that the grass could not grow upon it. I would be bound to say those plotters knew whereabouts he would be going to pray: they knew the place where Daniel's prayer was wont to be made; and they were sure they should find him there at his usual hours. And now again he has

> a purpose firm,
> And dares to make it known.

There must have been great excitement in the city then: all Babylon knew that this man was not going to swerve. They knew very well that the old statesman was a man of iron will; and that it was not at all likely he would yield. The lions' den had few terrors to him. He would rather be in the lions' den with God, than out of it without Him. And it is a thousand times better, friends, to be in the lions' den with God, and hold to principle—than to be out of it, and have money, but no principle.

I venture to say that man Daniel was worth more than any other man Darius had in his empire—yes, worth more than forty thousand men who wanted to get him out of the way. He was true to the king. He prayed for him; he loved him; and he did for that king everything he could that did not conflict with the law of his God.

And now the spies rush off to the king, and cry,

"O Darius, live for ever! Do you know there is a man in your kingdom who will not obey you?"

"A man who won't obey me! Who is he?"

"Why, that man Daniel. That Hebrew whom you set over us. He persists in calling upon his God."

And the moment they mention the name of Daniel, a frown arises upon the king's brow; and the thought flashes into his mind: "Ah! I have made a mistake: I ought never to have signed that decree. I might have known that Daniel would never 'call' upon me. I know very well whom he serves: he serves the God of his fathers." So, instead of blaming Daniel he blames himself: instead of condemning Daniel he condemns himself. And then he casts about in his mind as to how he could manage to preserve him unharmed. All that day, if you could have looked into the palace, you would have seen the king walking up and down the halls and corridors, greatly troubled with the thought that this man must lose his life before the sun sets on that Chaldaean plain; for if Daniel were not in the lions' den by sundown the law of the Medes and Persians would be broken: and, come what will, that law must be observed and kept.

Darius loved Daniel; and he sought in his heart to deliver him. All day he sought for some plan by which he might save Daniel, and yet preserve the Median law unbroken. But he did not love Daniel as much as your King loved you: he did not love him as much as Christ loved us: for if he had he would have proposed to have gone into the lions' den in his stead. Let us remember that Christ "tasted death" for us.

You might have seen those officers going out to bind that old man with the white flowing hair: they march to his dwelling; and they bind his hands together. And those Chaldaean soldiers lead captive the man who a few hours before ranked next to the king; the noblest statesman Babylon had ever possessed. They guard him along the way that leads to the lions' den. Look at him as he is led along the streets. He treads with a firm and steady step, bearing himself like a conqueror. He trembles not. His knees are firm: they do not smite together. The light of heaven shines in his calm face. And all heaven is interested in that aged man. Disgraced down here upon earth, he is the most popular man in heaven. Angels are delighted in him: how they love him up there! He had stood firm; he had not deviated; he had not turned away from the God of the Bible. And he walks with a giant's tread to the entrance of the lions' den; and they cast him in. They roll a great stone to the mouth of the den; and the king puts his seal upon it. And so the law is kept.

Daniel is cast into the den; but the angel of God flies down, and God's servant lights unharmed at the bottom. The lions' mouths are stopped: they are as harmless as lambs. And if you could have looked into that den, you would have found a man as calm as a summer evening. I do not doubt that at his wonted hour of prayer he knelt down as if he had been in his own chamber. And if he could get the points of the compass in that den, he prayed with his face toward Jerusalem. He loved that city; he loved the temple: and probably with his face toward the city of Jerusalem, he prayed and gave thanks. And later on I can imagine him just laying his head on one of the lions, and going to sleep: and if that were so, no one in Babylon slept more sweetly than Daniel in the den of lions.

But there was one man in Babylon who had no rest that night. If you could have looked into the king's palace, you would have seen one man in great trouble. Darius did not have in his musicians to play to him that night. Away with music and singing! There was no feast that night: he could eat nothing. The servants brought him dainty food; but he had no appetite for it. He felt troubled: he could not sleep. He had put in that den of lions the best man in his kingdom; and he upbraided himself for it. He said to himself, "How could I have been a party to such an act as that?"

And early in the morning—probably in the grey dawn, before the sun has risen—the men of Babylon could have heard the wheels of the king's chariot rolling over the pavement; and King Darius might have been seen driving in hot haste to the lions' den. I see him alight from his chariot in eager haste, and hear him cry down through the mouth of the den: "O Daniel, servant of the living God, is thy God, whom thou servest continually, able to deliver thee from the lions?"

Hark! A voice gives answer—why, it is like a resurrection voice—and from the depths come up to the king's ear the words of Daniel: "O king, live for ever! My God hath sent his angel, and hath shut the lions' mouths, that they have not hurt me: forasmuch as before him innocency was found in me; and also before thee, O king, have I done no hurt."

The lions could not harm him. The very hairs of his head were numbered. I tell you, that whenever a man stands by God, God will stand by him. It was well for Daniel that he did not swerve. Oh, how his name shines! What a blessed character he was!

The king gives command that Daniel should be taken up out of the den. And, as he reaches the top, I fancy I see them embracing one another; and that then Daniel mounts the king's chariot, and is driven back with him to the royal palace. There were two happy men in Babylon that morning. Most likely they sat down at meat together, thankful and rejoicing.

"No manner of hurt was found upon him." The God who had preserved Shadrach, Meshach, and Abednego, in the fiery furnace, so that "no smell of fire had passed on them," had preserved Daniel from the jaws of the lions.

But Daniel's accusers fared very differently. So to speak, they "digged a pit for him; and are fallen into it themselves." The king orders that Daniel's accusers shall be delivered to the same ordeal. And they were cast into the den; "and the lions had the mastery of them, and brake all their bones in pieces or ever they came at the bottom of the den."

Young men, let us come out from the world; let us trample it under our feet; let us be true to God; let us stand in rank, and keep step, and fight boldly for our King! And our "crowning time" shall come by and by. Yes, the reward will come by and by; and then it may perhaps be said of one another, of us: "O man, greatly beloved!" Young men, your moral character is more than money, mark that! It is worth more than the honour of the world: that is fleeting, and will soon be gone. It is worth more than earthly position: that is transient, and will soon be gone. But to have God with you, and to be with God—what a grand position! It is an eternal inheritance.

THE SECOND COMING OF CHRIST

Preface

WHAT MR. MOODY DOES in this sermon, for the most part, is to answer those who wish to avoid the teaching of this truth, and then attempt to elicit from the Scriptures what they have to say about our Lord's return. There actually are not what we call illustrations in this sermon, with the exception of an incidental reference to the writings of Dean Alford and a passing reference to something Mr. Moody had heard Newman Hall say. While Mr. Moody does not introduce a great number of illustrations here, he does bring in many relevant texts; and in the text of the brochure in which this sermon is printed, he ends by quoting nine different texts, which he introduces with the statement: "Now I want to give you some texts to study." In the brochure text that I have, the sermon is introduced by the quoting of a long poem beginning "I'm Waiting for the Lord," and after the sermon a long poem is quoted covering five pages beginning

> It may be in the evening,
> When the work of the day is done.

No name is attached to either of these poems.

Sometimes Mr. Moody has been criticized for preaching too often on the second coming of Christ. I think the criticism is altogether unjustified. This particular sermon I have only found in two volumes, *Gospel Awakening* (1879), pp. 660-70; and *To All People* (1877), pp. 499-514. There is another sermon entitled "Jesus Fulfilling Prophecy" also in *Gospel Awakening*, pp. 649-54. Mr. Moody often referred to the Lord's return, but it was not the subject of any frequently preached sermon. The brochure form of the sermon that I happened to have, extending to twenty-seven pages, bears the date of 1877 and was published in London. There is a discussion on the return of the Lord in *Moody: His Words, Works, and Workers*, W. H. Daniels, ed., pp. 467-78; in E. L. Pell, *Dwight L. Moody*, pp. 508-17; and in a volume of sermons by various clergymen, *The Second Coming of Christ*, pp. 16-32.

188 *The Best of D. L. Moody*

The Second Coming of Christ

In 2 Timothy 3:16, Paul declares: "All scripture is given by inspiration of God, and is profitable for doctrine, for reproof, for instruction in righteousness"; but there are some people who tell us, when we take up prophecy, that it is all very well to be believed, but that there is no use in one trying to understand it; these future events are things that the Church does not agree about, and it is better to let them alone, and deal only with those prophecies which have already been fulfilled. But Paul doesn't talk that way; he says: "All scripture is . . . profitable for doctrine." If these people are right, he ought to have said, "Some Scripture is profitable; but you can't understand the prophecies, so you had better let them alone." If God didn't mean to have us study the prophecies, he wouldn't have put them into the Bible. Some of them are fulfilled, and He is at work fulfilling the rest, so that if we do not see them all completed in this life, we shall in the world to come.

I don't want to teach anything dogmatically, on my own authority; but to my mind this precious doctrine—for such I must call it—of the return of the Lord to this earth is taught in the New Testament as clearly as any other doctrine in it; yet I was in the Church fifteen or sixteen years before I ever heard a sermon on it. There is hardly any church that doesn't make a great deal of baptism, but in all of Paul's epistles I believe baptism is only spoken of thirteen times, while it speaks about the return of our Lord fifty times; and yet the Church has had very little to say about it. Now, I can see a reason for this;

The Devil Does Not Want Us to See This Truth,

for nothing would wake up the Church so much. The moment a man takes hold of the truth that Jesus Christ is coming back again to receive His followers to Himself, this world loses its hold upon Him. Gas stocks and water stocks and stocks in banks and railroads are of very much less consequence to him then. His heart is free, and he looks for the blessed appearing of his Lord, who, at His coming, will take him into His blessed Kingdom.

In 2 Peter 1:20, we read: "No prophecy of the scripture is of any private interpretation." Some people say, "Oh, yes, the prophecies are all well enough for the priests and doctors, but not for the rank and file of the Church." But Peter says, "The prophecy came not by the will of man: but holy men spake as they were moved by the Holy Ghost," and those men are the very ones who tell us of the return of our Lord. Look at Daniel 2:45, where he tells the meaning of that stone which the King saw in his dream, that was cut out of the mountain without hands, and that broke in pieces the iron, the brass, the clay, the silver, and the gold. "The dream is certain, and the interpretation thereof sure," says Daniel. Now, we have seen the fulfillment of that prophecy, all but the closing part of it. The kingdoms of Babylon and Medo-Persia and Greece and Rome have all been broken in pieces, and now it only remains for this stone, cut out of the mountain without hands, to smite the image and break it in pieces till it becomes like the dust of the summer threshing-floor, and for this stone to become a great mountain and fill the whole earth.

BUT HOW IS HE GOING TO COME?

We are told how he is going to come. When those disciples stood looking up into heaven at the time of His ascension, there appeared two angels, who said unto them (Acts 1:11) : "Ye men of Galilee, why stand ye gazing up into heaven? This same Jesus which is taken up from you into heaven, shall so come in like manner as ye have seen him go into heaven." How did He go up? He took his flesh and bones up with Him. "Look at me; handle me; a spirit has not flesh and bones as ye see me have." I am the identical one whom they crucified and laid in the grave. Now I am risen from the dead and am going up to heaven. He is gone, say the angels, but He will come again just as He went. An angel was sent to announce His birth of the Virgin; angels sang of His advent in Bethlehem; an angel told the women of His resurrection, and two angels told the disciples of His coming again. It is the same testimony in all these cases.

I don't know why people should not like to study the Bible, and find out all about this precious doctrine of our Lord's return.

Some have gone beyond prophecy, and tried to tell the very day He would come. Perhaps that is one reason why people don't believe this doctrine. He is coming; we know that; but just when He is coming we don't know. Matthew 24:36 settles that. The angels don't know, that is something the Father keeps to Himself. If Christ had said, "I will not come back for 2,000 years," none of His disciples would have begun to watch for Him, until the time was near, but it is

The Proper Attitude of a Christian

to be always looking for his Lord's return. So God does not tell us when He is to come, but Christ tells us to watch. In this same chapter we find that He is to come unexpectedly and suddenly. In the twenty-seventh verse, we have these words, "For as the lightning cometh out of the east, and shineth even unto the west; even so shall also the coming of the Son of Man be." And again in the forty-fourth verse, "Therefore be ye also ready: for in such an hour as ye think not the Son of man cometh."

Some people say that means death; but the Word of God does not say it means death. Death is our enemy, but our Lord hath the keys of Death; He has conquered death, hell and the grave, and at any moment He may come to set us free from death, and destroy our last enemy for us; so the proper state for a believer in Christ is waiting and watching for our Lord's return.

In the last chapter of John there is a text that

Seems to Settle This Matter.

Peter asks the question about John, "Lord, what shall this man do? Jesus said unto him, If I will that he tarry *till I come,* what is that to thee? Follow thou me. Then went this saying abroad among the brethren, that that disciple *should not die.*" They did not think that the coming of the Lord meant death; there was a great difference between these two things in their minds. Christ is the Prince of Life; there is no death where He is; death flees at His coming; dead bodies sprang to life when He touched them or spoke to them. His coming is not death; He is the resurrection and the life; when He sets up His kingdom there is to be no death, but life forevermore.

There is another mistake, as you will find if you read your Bibles carefully. Some people think that at the coming of Christ everything is to be all done up in a few minutes: but I do not so understand it. The first thing He is to do is to take His Church out of the world. He calls the Church His bride, and He says He is going to prepare a place for her. We may judge, says one, what a glorious place it will be from the length of time He is in preparing it, and when the place is ready He will come and take the Church to Himself.

In the closing verses of the fourth chapter of 1 Thessalonians, Paul says: "If we believe that Jesus died and rose again, even so them also which sleep in Jesus will God bring with him . . . we which are alive and remain unto the coming of. the Lord shall not prevent them which are asleep. For the Lord Himself shall descend from heaven with a shout, with the voice of the archangel, and with the trump of God, and the dead in Christ shall rise first. Then we which are alive and remain shall be caught up together with them in the clouds, to meet the Lord in the air: and so shall we ever be with the Lord. Wherefore comfort one another with these words." That is, the comfort of the Church. There was a time when I used to mourn that I should not be alive in the millennium; but now

I Expect to Be in the Millennium.

Dean Alford says—almost everybody bows to him in the matter of interpretation—that he must insist that this coming of Christ to take His Church to Himself in the clouds, is not the same event as His coming to judge the world at the last day. The deliverance of the Church is one thing, judgment is another.

Now, I can't find any place in the Bible where it tells me to wait for signs of the coming of the millennium, as the return of the Jews and such like; but it tells me to look for the coming of the Lord; to watch for it; to be ready at midnight to meet Him, like those five wise virgins. The trump of God may be sounded, for any thing we know, before I finish this sermon—at any rate we are told that He will come, and at an hour when many look not for Him.

Some of you may shake your heads and say, "Oh, well, that is too deep for the most of us; such things ought not to be said before these young converts; only the very wisest characters, such as the ministers and the professors in the theological seminaries can understand them." But, my friends, you find that Paul wrote about these things to those young converts among the Thessalonians, and he tells them to comfort one another with these words. Here in the first chapter of 1 Thessalonians, Paul says: "Ye turned to God from idols to serve the living and true God; and to wait for His Son from heaven, whom he raised from the dead, even Jesus, which delivered us from the wrath to come." To wait for His Son; that is the true attitude of every child of God. If he is going to do that he is ready for the duties of life, ready for God's work; aye, that makes him feel that he is just ready to begin to work for God. Then over in the next chapter (1 Thessalonians 2:19), he says: "For what is our hope, or joy, or crown of rejoicing? Are not even ye in the presence of our Lord Jesus Christ at his coming?" And again, in the third chapter, at the thirteenth verse: "To the end he may stablish your hearts unblameable in holiness before God, even our Father, at the coming of our Lord Jesus Christ with all his saints." Still again, in the fifth chapter and twenty-third verse: *"I pray God* your whole spirit and soul and body be preserved blameless unto the coming of our Lord Jesus Christ." He has something to say about this same thing in every chapter; indeed, I have thought this Epistle to the Thessalonians might be called the Gospel of Christ's coming again.

There are

THREE GREAT FACTS

foretold in the Word of God. First, that Christ should come; that has been fulfilled. Second, that the Holy Ghost should come; that was fulfilled at Pentecost, and the Church is able to testify to it by its experience of His saving grace. Third, the return of our Lord again from Heaven—for this we are told to watch and wait "till He come." Look at that account of the last hours of Christ with His disciples. What does Christ say to them? If I go away I will send death after you to bring you to Me? I will send an angel after you? Not at all. He says: "I will come again, and receive you unto myself." If my wife were in a foreign country, and I had a beautiful mansion all ready for her, she would a good deal rather I should come and bring her to it than to have me send some one else to bring her. So the Church is the Lamb's wife. He has prepared a mansion for His bride, and He promises for our joy and comfort that

He Will Come Himself

and bring us to the place He has been all this while preparing.

It is perfectly safe to take the Word of God just as we find it. If He tells us to watch, then watch! If He tells us to pray, then pray! If He tells us He will come again, wait for Him! Let the Church bow to the Word of God, rather than try to find out how these things can be. "Behold, I come quickly," said Christ. "Even so come, Lord Jesus," should be the prayer of the Church.

Take the account of the words of Christ at the communion table. It seems to me the devil has covered up the most precious thing about it. "For as often as ye eat this bread, and drink this cup, ye do show forth the Lord's death *till he come.*" But most people seem to think that the Lord's table is the place for self-examination and repentance, and making good resolutions. Not at all; you spoil it that way; it is to show forth the Lord's death, and we are to keep it up till He comes.

Some people say, "I believe Christ will come on the other side of the millennium." Where do you get it? I can't find it. The Word of God nowhere tells me to watch and wait for the coming of the millennium, but for the coming of the Lord. I don't find any place where God says the world is to grow better and better, and that Christ is to have a spiritual reign on earth of a thousand years. I find that

The World Is to Grow Worse and Worse,

and that at length there is going to be a separation. "Two women grinding at the mill; one taken and the other left. Two men in one bed; one taken and the other left." The Church is to be translated out of the world, and of this we have two examples already, two representatives as we might say in Christ's Kingdom, of what is to be done for all His true believers. Enoch is the representative of the first dispensation, Elijah of the second, and, as a representative of the third dispensation, we have the Saviour Himself, who is entered into the heavens for us, and became the first fruits of them that slept. We are not to wait for the great white throne judgment, but the glorified Church is set on the throne with Christ, and to help to judge the world.

Now, some of you think this is a new and strange doctrine, and that they who preach it are speckled birds. But let me tell you that many spiritual men in the pulpits of Great Britain are firm in this faith. Spurgeon preaches it. I have heard Newman Hall say that he knew no reason why Christ might not come before he got through with his sermon. But in certain wealthy and fashionable churches, where they have the form of godliness, but deny the power thereof,—just the state of things which Paul declares shall be in the last days,—this doctrine is not preached or believed. They do not want sinners to cry out in their meeting, "What must I do to be saved?" They want intellectual preachers who will cultivate their taste, brilliant preachers who will rouse their imagination, but they don't want the preaching that has in it the power of the Holy Ghost. We live in the day of

SHAMS IN RELIGION.

The Church is cold and formal; may God wake us up! And I know of no better way to do it than to get the Church to looking for the return of our Lord.

Some people say, "Oh, you will discourage the young converts if you preach that doctrine." Well, my friends, that hasn't been my experience. I have felt like working three times as hard ever since I came to understand that my Lord was coming back again. I look on this world as a wrecked vessel. God has given me a life-boat, and said to me, "Moody, save all you can." God will come in judgment to this world, but the children of God don't belong to this world; they are in it, not of it, like a ship in the water. This world is getting darker and darker; its ruin is coming nearer and nearer; if you have any friends on this wreck unsaved, you had better lose no time in getting them off. But some one will say, "Do you then make the grace of God a failure?" No; grace is not a failure, but man is. The antediluvian world was a failure; the Jewish world was a failure; man has been a failure everywhere, when he has had his own way and been left to himself. Christ will save His Church, but He will save them finally by taking them out of the world. Now, don't take my word for it; look this doctrine up in your Bibles, and, if you find it there, bow down to it, and receive it as the word of God. Take Matthew 24:50: "The lord of that servant shall come when he looketh not for him, and in an hour that he is not aware of, and shall cut him asunder, and appoint him his portion with the hypocrites: there shall be weeping and gnashing of teeth." Take 2 Peter, third chapter, third and fourth verses: "There shall come in the last days scoffers, walking after their own lusts, and saying, Where is the promise of his coming? for since the fathers fell asleep, all things continue as they were from the beginning of the creation." Go out on the streets of this city, and ask men about the return of our Lord, and that is just what they would say: "Ah, yes; the Lord delayeth His coming!"

"Behold, I come quickly," said Christ to John, and the last prayer in the Bible is, "Even so, Lord Jesus, come quickly." Were the early Christians disappointed, then? No; no man is disappointed who obeys the voice of God. The world waited for the first coming of the Lord, waited for 4,000 years, and then He came. He was here only thirty-three years, and then He went away. But He left us a promise that He would come again; and, as the world watched and waited for His first coming and did not watch in vain, so now, to them who wait for His appearing, shall He appear a second time unto salvation. Now, let the question go round, "Am I ready to meet the Lord if He comes to-night?" "Be ye also ready, for in such an hour as ye think not the Son of Man cometh."

There is another thought I want to call your attention to, and that is: Christ will

Bring All Our Friends with Him

when He comes. All who have died in the Lord are to be with Him when He descends from His Father's throne (Revelation 3:21) into the air. 1 Thessalonians 4:16, 17. A brief interval of time ensues between this meeting of all His saints in the air and His coming with all his saints to execute judgment upon the ungodly, to chain Satan in the bottomless pit for the thousand years, and to establish the millennial reign in great power and glory. "Blessed and holy is he that hath part in the first resurrection: on such the second death has no power, but they shall be priests of God and of Christ, and shall reign with him a thousand years." (Revelation 20:6). "But the rest of the dead lived not again until the thousand years were finished. This is the first resurrection" (verse 5). That looks as if the Church was to reign a thousand years with Christ before the final judgment of the great White Throne, when Satan shall be cast into the Lake of Fire, and there shall be new heavens and a new earth. Revelation 20:1-15; 21:1-5.

HEAVEN AND WHO ARE THERE

Preface

MR. MOODY PROBABLY PREACHED on the subject of heaven, with different emphases, more frequently than on any other one subject in his long ministry. This particular text is the first of two sermons on heaven appearing in *Great Joy*. It is significant that no scripture is given until Mr. Moody is far into his sermon, and then, surprisingly, he begins with quotations from 2 Chronicles and 1 Kings. The sermon is filled with illustrations, at least ten of them, and, contrary to what one would expect, the longer illustrations have to do with death. In two illustrations, mothers are at the point of death, another describes a soldier dying on the battlefield, another records the sad death of the son of a rich man, and the death of the boy of believing Presbyterian parents. With so many illustrations relating to death, some of them at great length, it is not surprising that there is very little attention given to a description of heaven itself, or even an attempted discussion of the Holy City at the conclusion of the book of Revelation.

This particular sermon will be found over and over again in Mr. Moody's published works, as in *Gospel Awakening* (1879), pp. 264-73; *Great Joy* (1879), pp. 73-93; *Great Redemption* (1889), pp. 320-50; *Holding the Fort*, pp. 228-38; *London Discourses* (1875), pp. 116-25; *Moody's Great Sermons* (1899), pp. 76-91; and *Sermons, Addresses, and Prayers* (1877), pp. 78-85. His sermon "Laying Up Treasures in Heaven," may be found in *Gospel Awakening*, pp. 274-84; *London Discourses*, 125-38; and *Sermons, Addresses, and Prayers*, pp. 86-94; as well as in Richard B. Cook, *Life, Work, and Sermons of Dwight L. Moody* (Baltimore, 1900), pp. 486-500. In a volume of his sermons, *Conversion, Service and Glory* (London: n.d.), six of his sermons on heaven are brought together, pp. 263-377, successively entitled "Its

Hopes," "Its Inhabitants," "Its Happiness," "Its Certainty," "Its Riches," "Its Rewards."

These sermons on heaven were often reprinted in book form as far back as 1877 when *Heaven, Two Addresses* was published in London. The book *Heaven and How to Get There* sold 325,000 copies in the last two decades of the nineteenth century. The book carrying the title *Heaven, Where It Is . . .* was first published in 1880 and went through many editions.

Various sermons on heaven by Mr. Moody also appeared in the following: E. L. Pell, *Dwight L. Moody* (1900), pp. 489-98; Charles F. Goss, *Echoes from the Pulpit and Platform,* pp. 440-57; *Laying Up Treasure,* pp. 125-38; two sermons in Richard B. Cook, *Life, Work and Sermons of Dwight L. Moody,* pp. 470-501.

Heaven and Who Are There

I WAS ON MY WAY to a meeting one night with a friend, and he asked, as we were drawing near the church, "Mr. Moody, what are you going to preach about?" "I am going to preach about Heaven," I said. I noticed a scowl passing over his face, and I said, "What makes you look so?" "Why, your subject of Heaven. What's the use of talking upon a subject that's all speculation? It's only wasting time on a subject about which you can only speculate." My answer to that friend was, "If the Lord doesn't want us to speak about Heaven, He would never have told us about such a place in the Scriptures; and, as Timothy says, 'All the Scriptures are given by inspiration, and all parts are profitable.'" There's no part of the Word of God that is not profitable, and I believe if men would read more carefully these Scriptures they would think more of Heaven. If we want to get men to fix their hearts and attention upon Heaven, we must get them to read more about it. Men who say that Heaven is a speculation have not read their Bibles. In the blessed Bible there are allusions scattered all through it. If I were to read to you all the passages upon Heaven from Genesis to Revelation, it would take me all night and tomorrow to do it. When I took some of the passages lately and showed them to a lady, "Why," said she, "I didn't think there was so much about Heaven in the Bible." If I were to go into a foreign land and spend my days there, I would like to know all about it; its climate, its inhabitants, their customs, their privileges, their government. I would find nothing about that land that would not interest me. Suppose you all were going away to Africa, to Germany, to China, and were going to make one of those places your home, and suppose that I had just come from one of those countries, how eagerly you would listen to what I had to say. I can imagine how the old, gray-haired men and the young men and the deaf would crowd around and put up their hands to learn something about it. But there is a country in which you are going to spend your whole future, and you are listless about what kind of a country it is. My friends, where are you going to spend eternity? Your life here is very brief. Life is but an inch of time; it is but a span, but a fibre, which will soon be snapped, and you will be ushered into eternity. Where are you going to spend it? If I were to ask you who were going to spend your eternity in Heaven to stand up, nearly every one of you would rise. There is not a man here, not one in Chicago, who has not some hope of reaching Heaven. Now, if we are going to spend our future there, it becomes us to go to work and find out all about it. I call your attention to this truth that Heaven is just as much a place as Chicago. It is a destination—it is a locality. Some people say there is no Heaven. Some men will tell you this earth is all the heaven we have. Queer kind of heaven this. Look at the poverty, the disease in the city; look at the men out of employment walking around our streets, and then say this is Heaven. How low a man has got when he comes to think in this way. There is a land where the weary are at rest; there is a land where there is peace and joy—where no sorrow dwells, and as we think of it, and speak about it, how sweet it looms up before us.

I remember soon after I got converted, a pantheist got hold of me, and just tried to draw me back to the world. Those men who try to get hold of a young convert are the worst set of men. I don't know a worse man than he who tries to pull young Christians down. He is nearer the borders of hell than any man I know. When this man knew I had found Jesus he just tried to pull me down. He tried to argue with me, and I did not know the Bible very well then, and he got the best of me. The only way to get the best of those atheists, pantheists, or infidels is to have a good·knowledge of the Bible. Well, this pantheist told me God was everywhere—in the air, in the sun, in the moon, in the earth, in the stars, but really he meant nowhere. And the next time I went to pray it seemed as if I was not praying anywhere or to any one.

We have ample evidence in the Bible that there is such a place as Heaven, and we have abundant manifestation that His influence from Heaven is felt among us. He is not in person among us; only in spirit. The sun is 95,000,000 miles from the earth, yet we feel its rays. In Second Chronicles we read: "If my people, which are called by my name, shall humble themselves, and pray, and seek my face, and turn from their wicked ways; then will I hear from heaven, and will forgive their sin, and will heal their land." Here is one reference, and when it is read, a great many people might ask: "How far is Heaven away? Can you tell us that?" I don't know how far it is away, but there is one thing I can tell you. He can hear prayer as soon as the words are uttered. There has not been a prayer said that He has not heard; not a tear shed that He has not seen. We don't want to learn the distance. What we want to know is that God is there, and Scripture tells us that. Turn to First Kings and we read: "And hearken thou to the supplication of thy servant, and of thy people Israel, when they shall pray toward this place: and hear thou in heaven thy dwelling place: and when thou hearest, forgive." Now, it is clearly taught in the Word of God that the Father dwells there. It is His dwelling-place, and in Acts we see that Jesus is there too. "But he, being full of the Holy Ghost, looked up stedfastly into heaven, and saw the glory of God, and Jesus standing on the right hand of God," and by the eye of faith we can see Him there to-night too. And by faith we shall be brought into His presence, and we shall be satisfied when we gaze upon Him. Stephen, when he was surrounded by the howling multitude, saw the Son of Man there, and when Jesus looked down upon earth and saw this first martyr in the midst of his persecutors, He looked down and gave him a welcome. We'll see Him by and by. It is not the jasper streets and golden gates that attract us to Heaven. What are your golden palaces on earth—what is it that makes them so sweet? It is the presence of some loving wife or fond children. Let them be taken away and the charm of your home is gone. And so it is Christ that is the charm of Heaven to the Christian. Yes, we shall see Him there. How sweet the thought that we shall dwell with Him forever, and shall see the nails in His hands and in His feet which He received for us.

I read a little story not long since which went to my heart. A mother was on the point of death, and the child was taken away from her in case it would annoy her. It was crying continually to be taken to its mother, and teased the neighbors. By and by the mother died, and the neighbors thought it was better to bury the mother without letting the child see her dead face. They thought the sight of the dead mother would not do the child any good, and so they kept it away. When the mother was buried and the child was taken back to the house, the first thing she did was to run into her mother's sitting-room and look all round it, and from there to the bed-room, but no mother was there, and she went all over the house crying, "Mother, mother!" but the child could not find her, and coming to the neighbor, said: "Take me back, I don't want to stay here if I cannot see my mother." It wasn't the home that made it so sweet to the child. It was the presence of the mother. And so it is not Heaven that is alone attractive to us; it is the knowledge that Jesus, our leader, our brother, our Lord, is there.

And the spirits of loved ones, whose bodies we have laid in the earth, will be there. We shall be in good company there. When we reach that land we shall meet all the Christians who have gone before us. We are told in Matthew, too, that we shall meet angels there: "Take heed that ye despise not one of these little ones; for I say unto you, that in heaven their angels do always behold the face of my Father which is in heaven." Yes, the angels are there, and we shall see them when we get home.

He is there, and where He is, His disciples shall be, for He has said: "I go to prepare a place for you, that where I am, there ye may be also." I believe that when we die the spirit leaves the body and goes to the mansion above, and by and by the body will be resurrected and it shall see Jesus. Very often people come to me and say: "Mr. Moody, do you think we shall know each other in Heaven?" Very often it is a mother who has lost a dear child, and who wishes to see it again. Sometimes it is a child who has lost a mother, a father, and who wants to recognize them in Heaven. There is just one verse in Scripture in answer to this, and that is: "We shall be satisfied." It is all I want to know. My brother who went up there the other day I shall see, because I will be satisfied. We will see all those we loved on earth up there, and if we loved them here we will love them ten thousand times more when we meet them there.

Another thought. In the tenth chapter of Luke we are told our names are written there if we are Christians. Christ just called His disciples up and paired them off and sent them out to preach the Gospel. Two of us—Mr. Sankey and myself—going about and preaching the Gospel, is nothing new. You will find them away back eighteen hundred years ago, going off two by two, like Brothers Bliss and Whittle, and Brothers Needham and Stebbins, to different towns and villages. They had gone out, and there had been great revivals in all the cities, towns, and villages they had entered. Everywhere they had met with the greatest success. Even the very devils were subject to them. Disease had fled before them. When they met a lame man they said to him, "You don't want to be lame any longer," and he walked. When they met a blind man they but told him to open his eyes, and behold, he could see. And they came to Christ and rejoiced over their great success, and He just said to them, "I will give you something to rejoice over. Rejoice that your names are written in Heaven." Now there are a great many people who do not believe in such an assurance as this: "Rejoice, because your names are written in heaven." How are you going to rejoice if your names are not written there? While speaking about this some time ago, a man told me we were preaching a very ridiculous doctrine when we preached this doctrine of assurance. I ask you in all candor, what are you going to do with this assurance if we don't preach it? It is stated that our names are written there; blotted out of the Book of Death and transferred to the Book of Life.

I remember, while in Europe, I was traveling with a friend—she is in this hall to-night. On one occasion, we were journeying from London to Liverpool, and the question was put as to where we would stop. We said we would go to the North-western, at Lime street, as that was the hotel where Americans generally stopped at. When we got there the house was full; could not let us in. Every room was engaged. But this friend said, "I am going to stay here, I engaged a room ahead. I sent a telegram on." My friends, that is just what the Christians are doing—sending their names in ahead. They are sending a message up saying: "Lord Jesus, I want one of those mansions You are preparing; I want to be there." That's what they're doing. And every man and woman here who wants one, if you have not already got one, had better make up your mind. Send your names up now. I would rather a thousand times have my name written in the

Lamb's Book than have all the wealth of the world rolling at my
feet. A man may get station in this world—it will fade away; he
may get wealth, but it will prove a bauble—"What shall it profit
a man if he gain the whole world and lose his own soul?" It is a
solemn question, and let it go around the hall to-night: "Is my
name written in the Book of Life?" I can imagine that man
down there saying, "Yes; I belong to the Presbyterian Church;
my name's on the church's books." It may be, but God keeps
His books in a different fashion than that in which the church
records of this city are kept. You may belong to a good many
churches; you may be an elder or a deacon, and be a bright light
in your Church, and yet you may not have your name written in
the Book of Life. Judas was one of the twelve, and yet he hadn't
his name written in the Book of Life. Satan was among the elect
—he dwelt among the angels, and yet he was cast from the high
hallelujahs. Is your name written in the Book of Life? A man
told me, while speaking upon this subject, "That is all nonsense
you are speaking." And a great many men here are of the same
opinion; but I would like them to turn to Daniel, twelfth chapter,
"And there shall be a time of trouble, such as never was since
there was a nation even to that same time: and at that time thy
people shall be delivered, every one that shall be found written
in the book." Every one shall be delivered whose names shall be
found written in the Book. And we find Paul, in the letters
which he wrote to the Philippians, addressing them as those "dear
yokefellows, whose names were written in the Book of Life." If
it is not our privilege to know that our names are written in the
Book of Life, here is Paul sending greetings to his yokefellows,
"whose names were written in the Book." Let us not be deceived
in this. We see it too plainly throughout the Holy Word. In
the chapter of Revelation which we have just read, we have three
different passages referring to it, and in the twenty-seventh verse,
almost the last words in the Scriptures, we read: "And there
shall in no wise enter into it any thing that defileth, neither whatsoever worketh abomination, or maketh a lie: but they which
are written in the Lamb's book of life." My friends, you will
never see that city unless your names are written in that Book
of Life. It is a solemn truth. Let it go home to every one, and

sink into the hearts of all here to-night. Don't build your hopes on a false foundation; don't build your hopes on an empty profession. Be sure your name is written there. And the next thing after your own names are written there, is to see that the names of the children God has given you, are recorded there. Let the fathers and mothers assembled to-night hear this and take it to their hearts. See that your children's names are there. Ask your conscience if the name of your John, your Willie, your Mary, your Alice—ask yourselves whether their names are recorded in the Book of Life. If not, make it the business of your life, rather than to pile up wealth for them; make it the one object of your existence to secure for them eternal life, rather than to pave the way to their death and ruin.

I read some time ago of a mother in an Eastern city who was stricken with consumption. At her dying hour she requested her husband to bring the children to her. The oldest one was brought first, and she laid her hand on his head and gave him her blessing and dying message. The next one was brought, and she gave him the same; and one after another came to her bedside until the little infant was brought in. She took it and pressed it to her bosom, and the people in the room, fearing that she was straining her strength, took the child away from her. As this was done she turned to the husband and said, "I charge you, sir, bring all those children home with you." And so God charges us. The promise is to ourselves and to our children. We can have our names written there, and then, by the grace of God, we can call our children to us and know that their names are also recorded there. That great roll is being called, and those bearing the names are summoned every day—every hour; that great roll is being called to-night, and if your name were shouted, could you answer with joy? You have heard of a soldier who fell in our war. While he lay dying, he was heard to cry, "Here! Here." Some of his comrades went up to him, thinking he wanted water, but he said, "They are calling the roll of Heaven, and I am answering," and in a faint voice he whispered "Here!" and passed away to Heaven. If that roll was called to-night, would you be ready to answer, "Here!" I am afraid not. Let us wake up; may every child of God wake up to-night. There is work to do.

Fathers and mothers, look to your children. If I could only speak to one class, I would preach to parents, and try to show them the great responsibility that rests upon them—try to teach them how much more they should devote their lives to secure the immortal treasure of Heaven for their children, than to spend their lives in scraping together worldly goods for them.

There is a man living on the bank of the Mississippi River. The world calls him rich, but if he could call back his first-born son he would give up all his wealth. The boy was brought home one day unconscious. When the doctor examined him he turned to the father, who stood at the bedside, and said, "There is no hope." "What!" exclaimed the father. "Is it possible my boy has got to die?" "There is no hope," replied the doctor. "Will he not come to?" asked the father. "He may resume consciousness, but he cannot live." "Try all your skill, doctor; I don't want my boy to die." By and by the boy regained a glimmering of consciousness, and when he was told that his death was approaching, he said to his father, "Won't you pray for my lost soul, father? You have never prayed for me." The old man wept. It was true. During the seventeen years that God had given him his boy he had never spent an hour in prayer for his soul, but the object of his life had been to accumulate wealth for that first-born. Am I speaking to a prayerless father or mother to-night? Settle the question of your soul's salvation and pray for the son or daughter God has given you.

But I have another anecdote to tell. It was Ralph Wells who told me of this one. A certain gentleman had been a member of the Presbyterian Church. His little boy was sick. When he went home his wife was weeping, and she said, "Our boy is dying. He has had a change for the worse. I wish you would go in and see him." The father went into the room and placed his hand on the brow of his dying boy, and could feel that the cold, damp sweat was gathering there; that the cold, icy hand of death was feeling for the cords of life. "Do you know, my boy, that you are dying?" asked the father. "Am I? Is this death? Do you really think I am dying?" "Yes, my son, your end on earth is near." "And will I be with Jesus to-night, father?" "Yes, you will be with the Saviour." "Father, don't you weep, for when I get there

I will go right straight to Jesus and tell Him you have been trying all my life to lead me to Him." God has given me two little children, and ever since I can remember I have directed them to Christ, and I would rather they carried this message to Jesus—that I had tried all my life to lead them to Him—than have all the crowns of the earth; and I would rather lead them to Jesus than give them the wealth of the world. If you have got a child, go and point the way. I challenge any man to speak of Heaven without speaking of children. "For of such is the kingdom of heaven." Fathers and mothers and professed Christians ignore this sometimes. They go along themselves and never try to get any to Heaven with them. Let us see to this at once, and let us pray that there may be many names written in the Lamb's Book of Life to-night.

"BE YE ALSO READY"

Preface

WHILE MR. MOODY OFTEN SPOKE of death and used scores of illustrations from deathbed scenes, his attendance at funerals is rarely referred to by his biographers. Three deaths greatly moved the evangelist—that of his brother in 1876, that of his mother in 1896, and the tragic death of Mr. and Mrs. Bliss in 1876. I have never seen any account of any message that Mr. Moody gave at the funeral of his mother, but his moving message at the funeral of his brother based upon John 1:41 appeared in a number of volumes, for example, *Gospel Awakening* (1879), pp. 39-94; *Great Joy* (1879), pp. 52-59; *Sermons, Addresses, and Prayers* (1877), pp. 46-51; and *To All People* (1877), pp. 339-42. This sermon preached the Sunday after the death of Mr. Bliss has, as fas as I know, only been published once, in the large volume of over 850 pages, *The Gospel Awakening*, edited by L. P. Remlap, published in Chicago in 1877. I am including the sermon here for two reasons.

In the first place, it is a remarkable illustration of the great gift Mr. Moody had of using current events to press home the need for men and women to accept Jesus Christ as their Saviour. Second, I know of no sermon of Mr. Moody's that has ever been printed in which the urgency of receiving Christ is pressed upon a congregation with so much fervor and earnestness as in these paragraphs. Even after a century we are still moved with this passionate plea, and it must have left a tremendous impression upon the thousands of people who gathered in the Chicago Tabernacle to hear Mr. Moody that Sunday afternoon. It is more free of illustrations than any sermon I have read of Mr. Moody's. In fact, apart from references to his brother's death, I find no real illustration here except the strange one beginning with the phrase that rarely ever passed Mr. Moody's lips, "There is a legend."

P. P. Bliss was born in Rome, New York, in 1838 and early revealed a remarkable talent for music, both instrumental and vocal. He came to Chicago in his early twenties, and soon served as leader of the choir of the very influential First Congregational Church of that city, and superintendent of its Sunday school. Residence in Chicago enabled him to meet Major Whittle, with whom he was to be intimately associated in gospel meetings on both sides of the Atlantic. In 1869 he met Mr. Moody. The two became devoted co-workers in the great campaigns that were soon to unfold. Mr. Bliss wrote such widely used songs as "Almost Persuaded," "Hold the Fort," "Jesus Loves Even Me," "Let the Lower Lights Be Burning," and edited the two principal editions of *Gospel Songs*. After visiting friends in Ohio, Mr. and Mrs. Bliss took a train for Chicago, on Friday night, December 29, 1876. About midnight this twelve-car train approached the shabbily constructed bridge across the Ashtabula River, and when once the weight of the entire train was felt, the bridge collapsed and dropped all the cars and their passengers seventy feet to a roaring river below. The bodies of these two devoted servants of Christ were never recovered, though there was an extensive search. Mr. Moody heard about the tragedy on Saturday, and this is the sermon that he preached on Sunday.

On the Death of Mr. P. P. Bliss

"Therefore be ye also ready," MATTHEW 24:44

I EXPECTED TO ENJOY, this afternoon, coming around here and hearing our friend Mr. Bliss sing the Gospel, and our friend Mr. Whittle preach. I was telling my wife, when I got home Friday night, that I was really glad I didn't have to work so hard on this Sabbath. I cannot tell you what a disappointment it has been to me. I have looked forward to those two men of God coming to this city. I had arranged and made my plans to stay over a few days, in order to hear and enjoy their services. Ever since I heard that I would have to take their place this afternoon, there has been just one text running in my mind. I cannot keep it out: "Therefore be ye also ready." You who have heard me preach the past three months, I think will bear witness to this, that I haven't said much about death. Perhaps I haven't been faithful in this regard. I'd always rather tell about life; perhaps there's not been warning enough in my preaching. But I feel that, if I should hold my peace this afternoon, and not lift up my voice and warn you to make ready for death, God might lay me aside and put some one else in my place; I must speak and forewarn you.

To-day has been one of the most solemn days in my life. The closing hours of every year, for the past ten or twelve years, have been very solemn to me. I think I never spent such a day as I have to-day. This world never seemed so empty, and men never looked so blind away from God, as they do to-day. It seems, as never before, that I cannot understand how life can go on in madness, how a man can keep away from Christ, when in just a stroke he is gone to eternity, and there is no hope. Those men I mean that really believe, intellectually, that the Bible is true; that if they die without regeneration, without being born again, they cannot see God's kingdom. How it is they can believe, and yet they can still stay away from Christ when such judgments are brought near to them, is a mystery to me. I hope the words of the Lord Jesus will find their way to your hearts, as they have to mine; I hope you will hear Him this afternoon saying: "Therefore, be ye also ready." He had been warning them; for in the verse preceding this text He said, "As in the days of Noah, they were eating and drinking, marrying and giving in marriage, until the flood came and took them all away." It came suddenly. How often the judgments of God come suddenly upon us. I want to call your attention to a few words we find in the Old Testament, in the 6th chapter of Jeremiah, at the 10th verse: "To whom shall I speak, and give warning, that they may hear? Behold their ear is uncircumcised, and they cannot hearken: behold, the word of the Lord is unto them a reproach; they have no delight in it." Also in the 33rd chapter of Ezekiel, 4th, 5th, and 6th verses: "Then whosoever heareth the sound of the trumpet, and taketh not warning; if the sword come, and take him away, his blood shall be upon his own head. He heard the sound of the trumpet, and took not warning; his blood shall be upon him. But he that taketh warning shall deliver his soul. But if the watchman see the sword come, and blow not the trumpet, and the people be not warned; if the sword come, and take any person from among them, he is taken away in his iniquity; but his blood will I require at the watchman's hand." Do you ask me, now, why I am so anxious to warn you? Because, if I don't, the blood of your soul will be required at my hand.

I want to warn you to-day; I want to plead with you to-day. And it is because I love you that I come to plead with you. I am sure there is nothing else that could induce me to speak this afternoon. I felt rather like going into my room and locking the door, and trying to learn what this providence means. I don't expect to find out yet; I'm not sure I'll ever know. But— (the speaker paused in deep emotion), I just felt I'd got to come down here this afternoon and cry out: "Therefore be ye also ready!" Make ready before the close of this sermon! Just ask yourselves this question, "Am I ready to meet God this moment?" If not, when will you be? God would not tell us to be ready, if He did not give us the power, unless it was something within our reach.

The thought is put into some of your minds that I am trying to take advantage of the death of this good man to frighten you and scare you; and I haven't any doubt Satan is doing this work, at this moment. Right here let me notice that some say I'm preaching for effect. That's what I am doing. I want to affect you; I want to rouse you out of your death-sleep, when I warn you to prepare to meet your God; for "in such an hour as you think not the Son of man cometh." It is just from pure love, pure friendship to you, that I warn you; the thought that I am trying to frighten you from selfish motives is from the pit of hell. You take a true mother; if she does not warn her child when playing with fire, you say she's not what she professes to be, not a true mother. If a father sees his boy going to ruin and don't warn him, is he a true father? I say, it is the single power of love that makes me warn you. Suppose I walk by a house on fire, with a man and woman in it, and their seven children. If I don't call out, hammer on the door, smash in the windows if necessary, and cry out, "Escape if you can," what would you say? You would say, I ought not to live. If souls are going down to death and hell all around me—I verily believe such live to-day, and some are in this building—how can I hold my peace, and not cry out at the top of my voice: "Therefore be ye also ready: for in such an hour as ye think not the Son of man cometh."

There is a legend, that I read some time ago, of a man who made a covenant with Death; and the covenant was this: that death should not come on him unawares—that death was to give warning of his approach. Well, years rolled on, and at last Death stood before his victim. The old man blanched and faltered out: "Why, Death, you have not been true to your promise; you have not kept your covenant. You promised not to come unannounced. You never gave me any warning." "How, how!" came the answer. "Every one of those gray hairs is a warning; every one of your teeth is a warning; your eyes growing dim are a warning; your natural power and vigor abated—that is a warning. Aha! I've warned you—I've warned you continually." And Death would not delay, but swept his victim into eternity.

That is a legend; but how many the past year have heard these warning voices. Death has come very near to many of us. What warnings have come to us all. The preacher's calls to repentance, how again and again they have rung in our ears. We may have but one or two more calls yet, this year, in the next few hours; but I doubt it. Then how many of us in the last twelve months have gone to the bedside of some loved friend, and kneeling in silent anguish unable to help, have whispered a promise to meet that dying one in heaven. Oh, why delay any longer! Before these few lingering hours have gone, and the year rolls away into eternity, I beg of you, see to it that you prepare to make that promise good. Some of you have kissed the marble brow of a dead parent this year, and the farewell look of those eyes has been, "Make ready to meet thy God." In a few years you will follow, and there may be a reunion in heaven. Are you ready, dear friends?

When visiting the body of my brother, just before he was put in the grave, I picked up his Bible, of the size of this in my hand; and there was just one passage of Scripture marked. I looked it up, and I found it read: "Whatsoever thy hand findeth to do, do it with thy might." As I read it that night, the hand that wrote it was silent in death. It was written in '76. Little did he think, when he wrote it, that in that same year he would be silent in the grave. Little did he think that the autumn wind and the winter snow would go roaring over his grave. Thank God, it was a year of jubilee to him! That year he found salvation; it was a precious year to his soul. That year he met his God. How often have I thanked God for that brother's triumphant death! It seems as though I could not live to think he had gone down to the grave unprepared to meet his God—gone without God and hope. Dear friends—dear unsaved friends—I appeal to you that you will now accept Christ. Seize the closing hours of this year; let not this year die till the great question is decided. I plead with you once more to come to the Lord Jesus. Oh, hear these blessed words of Christ, as I shout them again in your hearing: "Therefore be ye also ready."

Now death may take us by surprise. That's the way it has taken our dear friends, Mr. and Mrs. Bliss. Little did they know, as they rode toward Cleveland last Friday night, what was to be the real end of the journey. About the time I was giving out notice, last Friday night, of their being here this afternoon, they were then struggling with death. That was about the time they passed into glory-land. It was a frightful death, by surprise. But, beautiful salvation! Star of hope! In that time of gloom, darkness and death: they both were ready. They were just ripened for the kingdom of God. I do not think I ever saw two persons who have grown more in Christ than these dear friends have in the past four or five years. I do not think a man walks the streets of Chicago to-day who has so few enemies as P. P. Bliss. He was a man we will love in another world. When the summons came, it must have been terrible; it must have brought cruel pain for a few minutes. But it lasted only a few minutes, and—they were in glory. Only a few minutes—and they were all together in that world of light, perhaps raising the shout of praise, "Alleluiah, what a Saviour!" I think the heavenly choir has had a great accession to-day. I doubt whether many around the throne of God sing sweeter than P. P. Bliss. I doubt whether many have loved the Son of God more than he. With that golden harp of the glorified, how sweetly shall he sing!

But, my friends, while we are mourning here, are we ready? We cannot call them back. We may mourn for them; we may mourn for the sad misfortune that has befallen ourselves. But what is our loss is their gain. It is better for them there than here; it is better to be "absent from the body, and present with the Lord." Shall you join him in that blessed land? Say, are you ready?

Now there are three things which every man should be ready for in this world: ready for life, ready for death, and ready for judgment. Judgment after death is as sure as life; judgment is as sure as death. There are three sure things. "It is appointed unto man once to die, but after this the judgment." It is of very little account how we die, or where we die, if we are only prepared, if we are only ready. We don't know what may happen any day. It seems to me, we ought to be ready any hour, any moment; we know not what may happen any moment. Oh, let us get ready! It seems the sheerest folly to delay this matter a single moment. Look at that train, where great numbers were ushered into eternity unexpectedly. Little did they think that their time was so near at hand. Little did our friends, Mr. Bliss and wife, think that they were going to be ushered into eternity, as they stepped light-hearted on that railway train. It would seem that people ought to resolve never to step aboard a railway train again, until they're ready to meet their God. It would seem as though no one would lie down and go to sleep to-night, until he knows he is ready to meet the bridegroom.

Dear friends, are you ready? This question this afternoon, it seems to me, ought to go down into all our hearts. And then, if we are ready, we can shout over death and the grave; that death is overcome, the sting of death is gone, and the grave opens terrorless. Suppose we do go on and live thirty or forty years; it is all only a little moment. Suppose we die in some lone mountain, like Moses on Pisgah; or like Jacob, in the midst of our family; or like Joshua, with the leaders of Israel around us; or suppose God lets us die surrounded with the comforts and luxuries of home; or suppose death comes on unexpectedly and suddenly, as it did on Stephen; it may be we shall be called to die the death of the martyr, and be put to death unexpectedly; but if we are only ready, what care we just how our summons comes. If I am ready, I would as soon die like Stephen, or Moses on Pisgah. I would as soon die like our friend Mr. Bliss, as like Jacob with all his sons around him, if only I am ready for my glorious inheritance beyond the grave. That is the main question. It is not how we die. It is not where we die. At the worst, it may be but the sudden shock of a few minutes, and all will be over; and we enter upon eternal joy, joy for evermore. Millions and millions and millions of years in this world will not yield the joy of one minute of heaven. O my friends, shall you have a place in that heavenly home? Oh! will you not each one ask this question just now, "Am I ready, am I ready?"

I believe that every man in this Christian land has had some warning; some John the Baptist to warn him as Herod had, some Paul as Agrippa and Felix had, some friend like Nathan, sent to warn him, as David had; some friend to warn him such as Ahab had in Elijah. And, my friends, I think this is a day of warning to you. Are you not coming to God to-day? Will you not hear the Saviour's loving voice to-day, "Come unto me"? God will forgive your sins and blot them out, and give you a new heart. Oh, let not the sun go down to-night without being reconciled to God.

Little did those people on that train, as it neared Cleveland

Friday night, little did they think the sun was going down for them the last time, and that they should never see it rise again. It is going down to-night—as I am speaking, the last sun of the year; and some of you in this assemblage may never see it rise again. Dear friends, are you ready for the call, if it comes to you between now and to-morrow morning? This very night you may be called away; your soul may be required by God your Maker. Are you ready to meet the King and Judge of all the earth? Let me put, urgently but kindly, these questions to every soul here to-night. Can you say: "I have Christ; I have eternal life through Jesus Christ my Saviour"? If not, dear friends, let me ask you, what will you say when He shall come to judge you? If, this very night, He should summon you to stand before Him, what would you say?

Oh, how deceitful death is! Something may fall on us as we walk home to-night, or we may fall down and break some part of our body, and be ushered into eternity. We may be seized by some fit, and we're gone. We may have some disease around the heart, that is hidden from us and that we know nothing about, and this may be our last day on earth. "Boast not thyself of to-morrow"; we don't know what will happen, even before to-morrow. And then, another deception. A great many people, you know, because their parents have outlived the allotted years, because their parents were long-lived people, think that they're going to live long also. How many are deceived in that way. Then there is that lying deception: "Oh it is time enough to be a Christian—time enough to cry to God—when He calls us." Look at that wreck! Look at those people being dashed down that frightful chasm to frightful deaths! That is no time to get ready; that is not the time! They have all they can do trying to get out of the wreck,—bleeding, burning, drowning, frozen! How many in eternity in five minutes! How many instantly! No time for prayer in such chaos as that. I would not say God is not merciful; He may have heard even then, the penitent cry; but I would not dare to say, "Put it off till some calamity overtakes you." The word comes, now, at this moment, "Prepare to meet God," "Seek first the kingdom of God and his righteousness." Oh, that is the first duty and pleasure of life, not its last! It is more im-

portant than going home to look after the highest earthly affairs;
more important than if you could win the wealth and honors of
the universe! Let business be suspended and everything be laid
aside, until this greatest question of life—this greatest question of
time and eternity—is settled, "Prepare to meet thy God." Oh,
prepare!

My friends, I call upon you to come to the Lord Jesus Christ.
I call upon you to prepare this day and this hour to meet your
God. I lift up my voice, in warning, to all of this assembly. Would
you not rather be in the place of Mr. and Mrs. Bliss, and die as
they did, in that terrible wreck, by that appalling accident—
would you not rather choose that, than to live on twenty-five
years, or a hundred years, and die without God, and go down in
despair to dark rivers of eternal death! Oh, it was appalling!
But I would rather, a thousand times, have been on that train
that dark night, and taken that awful leap and met my God as
I believe Mr. and Mrs. Bliss have met Him, than to have the
wealth of worlds and die without God and hope! Oh, if you are
not ready, make ready just now! I think a great many tears
should be shed for the sins of the past year. If you take my advice,
you will not go out of this Tabernacle this night until you have
tasted repentance, and the joy of sins forgiven. Go into the
inquiry-room and ask some of the Christian people to tell you
the way of life, to tell you what to do to be saved. Say, "I want to
be ready to meet my God to-night; for I don't know the day or
the hour He may summon me."

I may be speaking to some this afternoon who are hearing
me for the last time. In a few days, I will be gone. My friends, to
you I want to lift up my warning voice once again. I want to
speak as to brethren beloved, hastening on to judgment: "Prepare to meet thy God." I beg of you, I beseech of you, this moment, don't let the closing hours, these closing moments of '76,
pass, until you are born of God, born of the Spirit, born from
death. This day, if you seek God, you shall find Him. This day,
if you turn from sin and repent, God is ready to receive you.
Let me say, He never will be more willing than to-day; and
you'll never have more power than to-day. If you are ready, He is
ready now to receive and bless you forever! Oh, may the God of

our fathers have compassion upon every soul assembled here!
May our eyes be opened; and all flee from the wrath to come!
May the divine warnings take hold on every soul! May we profit
by this sad calamity, and may many be raised up in eternity to
thank God that this meeting was ever held.

The Principal Texts of Mr. Moody's Printed Sermons

In ADDITION to Mr. Moody's sermons based on texts, there were a great number that were not related to a particular text, but to a particular subject, as "The Blood," "Enthusiasm," "Heaven," "The Holy Spirit," "What Christ Is to Us," "The Life and Character of Jacob." Then there were some sermons in which a number of texts were brought together, as for instance, the sermons on "The Beholds," "The Ten Comes," "The Four Great Questions from God," "The Eight I Wills of Christ."

Genesis
3:9
7:1
11:31-32
13:12
28:20-21
Leviticus
17:11
Deuteronomy
5:29
32:31
Joshua
1
1:6
1 Samuel
8:4
8:19
2 Samuel
15:19 ff.
1 Kings
18:2

18:21
21
2 Kings
5
Nehemiah
8:10
Job
19:25
Psalm
32
51
91
103:3-5
105
118:8
Ecclesiastes
11:6
Isaiah
4:6-7
13:3
26:4

32:2
33:24
49:24-25
53:4-5
55:3
55:6
Jeremiah
3:12
32:17
49:11
Daniel
1:8
5:25
5:27
9
11:32
12:2-3
Hosea
14:4
Matthew
5:14